Whatever happened to macro-economics?

M. H. Peston

Whatever happened to macro-economics?

Manchester University Press

© M. H. Peston 1980

Published by
Manchester University Press
Oxford Road, Manchester M13 9PL

British Library cataloguing-in-publication data

Peston, Maurice Harry
   Whatever happened to macro-economics?
   1. Macroeconomics
   I. Title
   339   HB171

ISBN 0-7190-0796-8

Set and Printed in Great Britain by
Express Litho Service (Oxford).

29638

Contents

Acknowledgements

I must first of all thank the economists at the University of Manchester for asking me to give the lectures on which this book is based, and for the welcome they gave me when they were delivered. I am particularly indebted to Professors M. J. Artis, D. J. Coppock and I. W. Steedman for taking the chair at successive lectures, and for the kind words they uttered at the time; although this does not commit them to agreeing with what I had to say.

Secondly, there is my debt to colleagues in the Department of Economics at Queen Mary College. In the dozen or so years that the Department has existed they have created an atmosphere of serious research and teaching; but have not allowed the excitement of professional argument to degenerate into unprofessional acrimony. Above all, I must thank Professor B. A. Corry, and Drs A. Coddington, D. A. Currie and E. Katz, from whose well known contributions to macro-economics I have benefited enormously.

Thirdly, I must thank the anonymous referee whose comments have enabled me to remove some, but not all, of the errors in the lectures as originally given. It was obvious that much of what I had to say he found most irritating, but this did not prevent him from making a number of useful and constructive comments.

The lectures themselves, of course, have been amended to only a small extent for publication. I am, therefore, extremely well aware of their limitations, especially in the brevity of their analysis of incomes policy and the behaviour of trades unions, and the balance of payments. None the less, I hope both students and colleagues will feel they are worth considering in the context of contemporary debate.

The book itself is dedicated to my wife, Helen.

M.P.

Queen Mary College
October 1979

Introduction

The chief purpose of this book is to consider at an extremely simple level the present state of macro-economic theory and macro-economic policy. It may also be regarded as a reaction to certain tendencies in macro-economics which, to say the least, I find rather puzzling.

One of these tendencies is the claim that there has emerged a new kind of macro-economics characterised by something called 'monetarism' which is supposed to represent an original contribution to the subject, and to mean the end of something called 'Keynesianism'. My view as stated here is that there is not a lot that is original in this approach to macro-economics, much of what it encompasses having been said earlier and better by other writers. Not least among these was Keynes himself, but Wicksell, Myrdal, Hayek and Robertson must also be mentioned in this context. Of course, economists have made original contributions in recent years, especially in the study of expectations, in the analysis of the relationship between stocks and flows, and in the exploration of the nature and significance of disequilibrium. But in large part this can best be seen as building on the writings of Keynes and his successors rather than destroying them.

A second tendency related to the first concerns the assumption of the self-equilibrating nature of the economic system and the role within it of the public sector. Keynes himself at the macro-economic level cast considerable doubts on whether the economy had an equilibrium at full employment.

He led economists to consider whether the system auto-matically and effectively tended to equilibrium when random shocks disturbed it. Since then the work of Patinkin has thrown some light on the question at the same level. Patinkin has produced some cogent arguments why the so-called real balance effect gives rise to some presumption in favour of the existence of a full employment equilibrium. But even this analysis is unconvincing about whether the real balance effect would generate a practicable path to equilibrium, let alone an efficient one.[1]

When it comes to general equilibrium in a disaggregated or micro-economic form, the position is even more difficult for those who wish to assume full employment. The existence of equilibrium has been proved for only the simplest of systems, far from everyday reality. Even in those cases there are serious problems for stability. On the basis of work at this level it cannot be assumed that the economy (or a convincing repre-sentation of it) has a non-trivial, unique, dynamically stable equilibrium.[2] In particular, the equilibrium defined by Professor Friedman to characterise the natural rate of unem-ployment may not exist and cannot be presumed to be stable.

This is not to say that the study of equilibrium is a waste of time, or that it is uninteresting to study economic problems based on a full employment assumption, or on the assumption (similar but not the same) that long-run real trends in the economy are independent of variations in monetary aggregates. As all of us repeat *ad nauseam,* Keynes was at pains to argue in the *General Theory* that, if full employment were guaranteed by the policy-maker, the economy would operate according to the classical theory. (In point of fact, this particular proposition has never been demonstrated by either classical economists or Keynesians.) But there is a world of difference between analysing the effects of a change in the government's demand for civil servants at full employment, and assuming that that is the only relevant case.

Both of these tendencies in economics have led to extremely tough questioning of the role of macro-economic policy, and especially fiscal policy.[3] It is argued that fiscal policy is unnecessary or impossible or unavoidably damaging. This is so because policy-makers are ignorant and their instruments too crude, or because the system is self-adjusting, individual decision-makers being as fully informed as possible, and the economy itself co-ordinating their actions in an unimprovable manner. Some protagonists of these views concede that the economy does not behave as well as we would like, but shake their heads sadly and avow that there is nothing we can do about it. Others find great advantages and benefits in periods of unemployment of labour and capital, which are alleged to have a cleansing function. Yet another group accept that effective stabilising policies exist but have the fatal flaw of destroying the decentralised private enterprise system on which prosperity (and even individual freedom itself) is based. (A variant of this group, but politically far distant from it, adopt a similar position, except that they welcome the fatal flaw.)

In the following pages it is argued that the case for fiscal policy can still be made. Certainly it has been subject to the most trenchant criticism, notably because earlier work did not fully comprehend the problem of the public sector borrowing constraint, on the one hand, and firms' and households' anticipation of and direct reaction to public policy, on the other. But to agree that policy-making has become more difficult does not imply that it has become impossible. *A fortiori,* no examination of the economic circumstances of the 1970s or the outlook for the 1980s could easily come to the conclusion that policy is unnecessary. Not only is the whole world crying out for successful macro-economic policies, but in the U.K. those politicians who philosophically aligned themselves with what might be termed 'policy passivism' are themselves no less active in the use of macro-economic instruments than those they decry.

Of course, the policy problem for the new decade sometimes appears insuperable, but then, every great problem appears insoluble until it is solved. In particular, even when (or perhaps mostly when) it seems obvious what should be done, it is hard to see what its intellectual foundations are. That was also true in the general slump, when the fiscal and monetarist advocates of expansion were right but their opponents had the best arguments and were the intellectually respectable establishment.

What, then, is there to be said of stagflation? The following appear to be the key aspects of this state of affairs:

1   A high rate of inflation.
2   A high rate of expected inflation.
3   A high rate of unemployment.
4   A low rate of growth of output.

If we ask what is meant by 'high', one answer for the first two of these is 'compared with zero' and another is 'compared with the average of the two post-war decades'. With respect to the third, 'high' may mean 'relative to full employment' or 'relative to the average of the two post-war decades'. With respect to the fourth, 'low' means either 'compared with the underlying rate of growth of capacity' or 'compared with the average growth rate of the two post-war decades'. In all cases I emphasise the period from the late 1940s to the late 1960s both because of the remarkable economic performance of the mixed economies of the world in this period, and because the question of what caused that performance has not yet been fully answered. There are those who believe the period was abnormal and transitory (although two decades can hardly be regarded as transitory except in the grandest sweep of history). Others take the precisely opposite view and regard those times as the norm, and what has happened since as an aberrant phenomenon which can still be dealt with. I myself argue below that there are good grounds for believing that the basic nature of the world's economy has changed in the 1970s, but that the new problems which confront us are not insoluble.

Assuming that stagflation is a correct characterisation of existing circumstances, why is an expansionary fiscal policy no longer said to be expansionary with respect to output? One answer to this question is that firms and households believe that eventually prices and also wages will rise. But that is to beg the question. Even if the long-run effect is correctly believed to be on prices, why is there no short-run effect on quantities?

A second answer to the question is that at existing levels of wage costs and market prices it does not pay firms to increase output and it does not pay households to increase the supply of labour. But, if that is the case, it seems to follow that the world economy is actually at full employment, and, therefore, that we are not in the midst of an inflationary recession.

The second answer sometimes goes hand in hand with the argument that an expansion in demand in one country largely spills over to other countries, and is met by foreign suppliers. One version of this sees these supplies as being directed from home demanders, so that again it appears to assume full employment. Alternatively, no such diversion occurs, and, therefore, it is accepted that there is excess world capacity. But the argument can hardly be applied to all countries unless for some peculiar reason all of them have suddenly developed a taste for foreign goods. It could, of course, more reasonably be applied to some of them, in which the relative price of home goods for exports is too high, and the price of tradables relative to incomes is too low. The conclusion follows none the less that some countries exist where firms and households in the aggregate are able and willing to meet an increased demand. It is, thus, not the case that an expansionary policy in those countries would have no output effect.

What is hard, if not impossible, to rationalise is the proposition that we are not at full employment (i.e. there is excess
supply of output and labour services available), but that an
expansion of demand only has price effects in the short term.
There is the obvious problem of leaving the state of the
economy pretty arbitrary (although some versions of Keynesian
theory are not immune from this criticism either). An
expansion of demand is alleged not to increase aggregate output, but a contraction of demand lowers it because of the
sticky nature of prices in the downward direction. Thus some
economists appeared bound to argue that for the short term
('short' being quite long in actual time), the economy is
simply forced to be where it actually is.

Although, in the Keynesian analysis of the problem, unemployment is due to deficient demand, the resulting state of
the economy may be one in which real wages are too high. An
expansionary fiscal policy, may, therefore, raise prices relative
to money wages as well as increasing output and employment.
In a stagflation a similar effect may be necessary: prices
received by firms may have to rise relative to wages paid by
them, or in dynamic terms the rate of increase of the former
may have to rise relative to the rate of increase of the latter.
If the rate of inflation is already excessive, governments may
fear the consequences of increasing that further more than
they object to unemployment. Thus they may decide not to
pursue an expansionary fiscal policy. But note that this is a
matter of choice, not feasibility. In an inflationary recession
they fear the inflation more than the recession, and therefore adopt policy measures to deal with the first of these even
though the result is to exacerbate the problem of the second.

My conclusion concerning expansionary policy is as follows:

1   In some countries real wage costs to the firm may have
    risen excessively, inhibiting an output response. In
    addition, tax changes may have been such that the after-tax
    wage received by workers is low (especially compared with

social security payments), inhibiting a supply response on their part.

2 In some countries there is genuine excess capacity in that firms are able and willing to meet increased demand and can get the necessary labour.

3 In many countries even with aggregate excess supply, domestic increases in demand spill over to a larger extent than heretofore to foreign suppliers.

The tax position, the greater difficulty of getting a real wage adjustment where it is needed, and an increased propensity to import mean that a country acting alone takes greater risks with an expansionary fiscal policy. In particular, it may generate more inflation for a given output increase. But this does not mean for the single country (and especially for those with low inflation rates and reasonably high productivity) that an expansionary fiscal policy must fail. It certainly does not mean that, for the world economy as a whole, expansionary fiscal policies must fail.

Beyond this I would argue that the nature of policy may have to change somewhat. The point has already been made about the value of international economic co-operation, although there is nothing new about that, since it was a central theme at Bretton Woods thirty-five years ago. Domestically, however, macro-economic policy must also be more co-operative and persuasive. Trade unions may have to be convinced about realistic bounds to income growth, firms may have to participate in a prices and incomes policy, and governments may be obliged to change the structure of taxes and benefits. But it is surely mistaken to conclude that 'fiscal policy is dead'.

Notes

[1] D. Patinkin. *Money, Interest and Prices* (Second edition, Harper and Row, 1965).

[2] A key reference is H. Scarf, 'Some examples of global instability of the competitive equilibrium' (*International Economic Review*, 1960).

[3] A valuable discussion of this question is to be found in A. Peacock and G. Shaw, 'Is fiscal policy dead?' (*Banca Nazionale del Lavoro Quarterly Review*, June 1978). There has also appeared since these lectures were given the excellent collection of essays edited by S. Cook and P. Jackson, *Current Issues in Fiscal Policy* (Martin Robertson, 1979).

Chapter One

I want to start with what I shall call, for want of a better name, the old macro-economics. Unfortunately there are a great many answers to the question 'What was the old macro-economics?'. I shall consider only a few of them — not surprisingly, those corresponding to my experience and interests. And even then, my discussion of them can only be a brief one.

The most straightforward answer to our simple question can be made up of two parts; (a) the income—expenditure model, and (b) the quantity theory model. They may be written as follows:

$$X = B\ \frac{A}{P} \qquad\qquad 1$$

$$X = V\ \frac{M}{P} \qquad\qquad 2$$

where X is real output, P is the price level, A is autonomous expenditure in money terms (which may include government expenditure), M is the quantity of money, B is the multiplier and V is the velocity of circulation of money. Using $*$ as a superscript to mean 'percentage change in' we may rewrite the equation as:

$$X^* = B^* + A^* - P^* \qquad\qquad 1.1$$

$$X^* = V^* + M^* - P^* \qquad\qquad 2.1$$

Now, I write these equations in this way in order to make an obvious point about their similarities. Although there has allegedly been a great debate going on in the past decade on the respective merits of so-called 'Keynesianism' and 'monetarism', at the most elementary level, from the methodological point of view, the theories are surprisingly similar.[1]

1   They are both highly aggregative.
2   They both multiply an exogenous variable to obtain the same endogenous variable, money income, itself a product of two index numbers: the scale of real output and the general price level. The variables themselves are observable and it is also possible to make direct estimates of the 'multipliers'.
3   Each views its 'multiplier' as being fixed on average in the short term, but capable of being varied by policy beyond that and also subject to secular change.
4   Each gives rise to simple and explicit predictions and policy advice.
5   While the models are static, it is easy to add some elementary dynamics to them. Firstly, there is no problem in writing them in rate of change form. Secondly, few difficulties arise in taking account of lagged values of output, prices, the quantity of money, and autonomous expenditure.
6   Because of many of the characteristics already listed, econometric estimation is facilitated. More generally, each approach is intrinsically empirical and can be related to historical experience.

Of course, this is not to say that the theories are exactly the same. The 'Keynes' theory asserts either that the price level is fixed, or that its rate of change is given and uninfluenced by the working of the model itself. The 'Quantity' theory asserts that real output is fixed, or that its rate of change is given and is not influenced by the working of the model itself. Thus the former may be criticised for having too little to say about prices, and the latter for having too little to say about real output.

Implicit in the former is some assumption of full employment or of an upper bound to output or its rate of expansion in normal conditions. Thus, treating the causal relationship as from A to X, it is taken for granted that as X approaches some critical value $\overline{X}$ or X^* some critical value $\overline{X}^*$, the effect of higher A on X or A^* on X^* tends to zero. In the latter approach, perhaps more debatably, there is an implicit assumption of a lower bound to the price level or its rate of change, again in normal conditions. Thus, viewing the causal relationships as from M to P, it will happen that as P approaches $\overline{P}$ or P^* approaches $\overline{P}^*$ the effects of lower M on P or lower M^* on P^* tends to zero.

To put this point succinctly, for certain circumstances the 'Keynesian' theory of output becomes a theory of prices and the 'Quantity' theory of prices becomes a theory of output. If it is accepted that X and P (or X^* and P^*) are both legitimately left-hand-side or dependent variables, each theory runs into the problem of distinguishing price effects from output effects, and must accept the criticism of being *ad hoc* when it does so.

This leads to some further points of comparison. Each of the theories may be criticised for paying too little attention to the analysis of behaviour. They are both extremely mechanical, assuming that human beings, whether organised in firms or in households, are unreflective and incapable of learning from experience. In addition, neither is sufficiently appreciative of the complexity of the control or policy problem.[2] One assumes, for example, that the authorities can operate directly on real government expenditure, and the other focuses on the quantity of money. These instruments can neither be varied as easily nor kept under as strict control as the policy measures typically advocated require. Those of us who are fine tuners

have exaggerated the facility with which this can be under-
taken.[3] But others who have pressed for tight control of public expenditure and the setting of rigid monetary targets have
also been obliged to recognise how difficult that turns out to
be. Both theories share a policy optimism, one claiming the
elixir of full employment, the other the remedy for inflation.
Again, it seems to me that the fact that they have this in
common is just as significant as their many differences. The
last point of similarity for the time being relates to the
labour market and the definition of full employment. It is
not doubted that the quantity theory has had connected with
it a theory of the labour market in which the supply of labour
was a function of the real wage (after tax and transfers paid
and received by the wage earner) and the demand for labour
was a function of the real wage (after tax and transfers paid
and received by the firm). An equilibrium was defined at that
real wage which equated demand and supply.

If the 'Keynesian' theory is that of Keynes's *General
Theory,* I think it is widely recognised that there too the same
demand and supply curves are postulated, and the same full
employment point is defined. Of course, it was not suggested
that the labour market was asserted to work in the same way
by the two sets of theorists, or that their views on the possibility of reaching full employment were the same.[4] But what
they meant by full employment was the same. (I must add *en
passant,* therefore, that it is wrong to assert that a central
postulate of the *General Theory* was money illusion if by that
is meant that workers mistake money wage increases for real
wage increases. The purpose of Keynes's peculiar definition of
involuntary unemployment was to emphasise the workers'
resistance to money wage cuts as a means to real wage cuts.
The reason they did not resist an increase in the price level of
wage goods was the vital one that that did not disturb relativities. If the workers were misled at all, therefore, it would
be by relativity illusion. And even that can be rationalised in

circumstances where unemployment is due to deficient demand with no need for relative price or wage changes in full equilibrium.)

Now, the income—expenditure model or the quantity theory model does not comprise the whole answer to our initial question. It may be readily admitted that they are not even by themselves an intellectually satisfactory part of the answer. The Keynesian would point out that his theory had a monetary side, and that the IS—LM apparatus, for example, is over three decades old. The quantity theorist would ask us not to neglect his discussion of investment and savings as functions of the rate of interest. But all that only serves to bring out the methodological similarities and the common approach even more. Indeed, since a Hicks or a Modigliani would claim that the two approaches can be integrated into a single one without contradiction, the conclusion emerges without room for argument at all that there was only one old macro-economics.

Let us not, however, pursue that theme, but turn to something else that could claim to be the answer to the question 'What was macro-economics?'. It is the econometric model, in its various guises from the large-scale model of hundreds of equations to the reduced form of just one. The former are like Frankenstein's monsters, understood at best by their makers, rather out of control, and terrifying to the rest of the profession. The latter also wield a strange power, and have a peculiar fascination, especially for journalists. Exceptionally good examples come to mind from the past couple of decades. To start with there was the Phillips curve, which supposedly told the exact degree of capacity utilisation that led to wages rising at the underlying rate of growth of capacity and hence to price stability. Then there was the two-year (but variable) lagged relationship between increases in the quantity of money and increases in the inflation rate. More recently, there has been the attempt to re-establish empirically purchasing power parity and justify the formula for exchange rates which states that they have to adjust to correspond to changes in relative price levels.

If we ask what have been the benefits of the econometric approach to macro-economics the following answers spring to mind:

1 It requires a specific formulation of the relationships to be tested.
2 It necessitates a definite commitment on what is cause and what is effect.
3 It obliges the researcher to give some consideration to the stochastic specification of the model being estimated.
4 It engenders a respect for the data being used, both as to their behaviour and as to their accuracy.
5 It clarifies the distinction between what is directly observed and what is not, and in the case of the former what is observed in numerical form and what is not.

But merely to list a number of points such as these is to realise how far econometrics in practice has fallen below the standards of scientific objectivity that ought to have been expected of it. Of course, a great deal that is useful has come out of the attempts to estimate both individual equations and complete models. To see whether the theory 'fits' the data is always interesting. To take an old example, the behaviour of real wages over the trade cycle represents a fundamental puzzle in the controversy over Keynes versus the classics. The contrast between cross-sectional and cyclical expenditure functions has led to many interesting advances in theory. More recently, the cyclical variation of quits, lay-offs, and new hirings, to say the least, rather complicates matters for several theorists.[5]

But, having said that, I am bound to say that too often the econometric approach and the econometric model in all its forms have been irrational and anti-intellectual. The stress on what fits or what can be made to fit, and the rejection of what is 'not supported by data' have brought empirical work into disrepute. In particular, I have two complaints. While appreciating the value of manipulating the data to get as good an estimate as possible, the critical spirit requires a certain even-handedness in discussing what fails to fit. From as far back as the time of the early Cowles Commission work, the reporting of successes (coupled with mention of a few failures) has been recognised as giving a serious bias to the interpretation of economic phenomena. This is not to suggest that the applied econometrist must attempt the logically impossible task of stating everything that is not the case. It is to press for more information on computational experiments that have failed.

This leads me to my second complaint, which is to point out that to the scientist the peculiar is at least as significant as the normal. (The two are, of course, dual to each other.) What fails to fit, what is puzzling, is quite likely to lead to the most important of intellectual breakthroughs. For the monetarist those years in which the inflation rate did not correspond to earlier behaviour of the money stock should be the ones that interest him most. For the Keynesian the cases in which increased effective demand did not call forth a multiplied increase in domestic output are the ones to concentrate on. For both it must be continually emphasised that the set of available data points is only a sub-set of all the variables in macro-economic theory. In addition, it has at least one natural arrangement, namely as a temporal or historical sequence.[6] This is not to say that the sequence in time always matters, rather to place some onus of justification on those who ignore it. In addition, the economy is made up of individual people organised in institutions and operating in markets. Theorists may be right to abstract from all this at the macro-level, and econometrists to give it no explicit role, but again it is proper to query those assumptions now and again.

I myself, with such institutional factors in mind as the rise of the trade union movement and the growing importance of the public sector, have argued that the earlier stability of the Phillips curve was 'more of a curiosity than a sign of the strength of some underlying structure'.[7] This is a theme I shall return to in Chapters II and III.

In this chapter, I must go to my third answer to the question of what macro-economics used to be. Macro-economics as seriously set out in Keynes's *General Theory*, but for the most part left out of elementary textbooks, and of much undergraduate teaching of economics, was a type of fundamental theory devoted to the central issue of how the economic system works as a whole. It was concerned with the analysis of the basic workings of a decentralised market capitalist system, with many complex financial institutions and with a sizeable but not overwhelming public sector. The markets were not all necessarily perfectly competitive (although Keynes himself tended to assume they were),[8] but they were to be regarded as the predominant means of resource allocation. This system was in a constant state of flux determined by changing external forces and its internal response to them. Its state at any time was the result of both the external and the internal dynamics, which would also determine what states it would proceed to next.

The fundamental questions that emerged were (and for the most part remain) unanswered:

1   Did the economy have a tendency towards some characteristic state, independent of the external forces at work or its precise dynamic response to them? Could this characteristic state be called full employment, or was there a chronic tendency towards unemployment?

2   Why did output and output-related variables show a cyclical tendency? Are cycles primarily due to cyclical behaviour of the exogenous variables or to the internal dynamics of the system? (There is also the question of whether in a proper sense the fluctuations of real output are cyclical, or is that a statistical mirage?)

3 Was inflation a characteristic state of the economy, a transitory condition, or again something chiefly connected with external factors?

4 What was the connection between all this behaviour and the market mechanism? Was it the decentralisation that was critical, or merely the private ownership of capital? Were there particular difficulties arising from the existence of financial markets, including those for foreign exchange? How vital was international trade?

5 How far was the problem of full employment one of dealing with or failing to cope with risk and uncertainty? Was there a special form of market failure consisting in not being able to buy and sell enough risks? Is it that Knightian uncertainty was the dominant feature of a social system within which individuals are free to choose, and that a decentralised economy can adjust only slowly if at all to its effects? Need any special emphasis be placed on the labour market?

There are some comments that must be made immediately. One is that even in conditions of widespread Keynesian unemployment the economy still continues to allocate resources using the price mechanism. There is less than full employment, and at the margin neither labour nor capital is scarce, but goods and services continue to be produced according to price relative to cost, and purchased according to relative prices and incomes. The price mechanism operates at less than full employment and out of full equilibrium. However, this is not the same as saying that this mechanism itself restores full employment and full equilibrium.

Consider classical theory in its normal formulation without a great deal of emphasis on particular institutions or the government. We have already remarked that this model has defined for it a full employment equilibrium, and, considering points of full equilibrium alone, behaviour and outcomes are determined by real factors. At any point of time the economy is subject to all manner of minor changes to which it adjusts, but these do not affect its macro-economic equilibrium. Thus an individual worker may decide to move home or a firm may try its hand competing in a new market. Broadly speaking, and confining ourselves to non-growth problems, aggregate demand and supply and their major components do not change significantly. All this is, moreover, compatible with the world looking pretty dynamic to the single firm or household. The micro-economic equilibrium of the economy may change while its macro-economic equilibrium is unaffected, This seems to me to be what classical and neo-classical general equilibrium theory is about. In the neighbourhood of equilibrium the economy is able to find its way, via a relative price mechanism, from one micro-economic equilibrium to another.

It is customary to confound this equilibrating process with one by which the economy adjusts to a shock which is macroscopic in scale and implying a shift in its macro-economic equilibrium state. My contention is that the problem of macroeconomic equilibrium is not the same as micro-economic general equilibrium, and that a presumption in favour of a decentralised search or implicit computation procedure leading to the latter does not imply a presumption in favour of the same procedure leading to the former. There is a world of difference between moving from one state to an equilibrium where the distance between the two is infinitesimally small, or 'very small', and moving when the difference is significantly large.[9]

To argue in this way requires us to make a distinction between shocks to the system according to their scale and according to their impact on full equilibrium (if we knew it as the perfect observer, so to speak, which, of course, in practice is an impossibility). I am not yet able to find a satisfactory definition of what is required, so that the ability to make the distinction must be seen as a working assumption. What I have in mind, however, is obvious, namely an analysis of the consequences of such shocks as a general change in the propensity to consume, the marginal efficiency of capital, the desired rate of increase in real wages on the part of workers, an increase in the price of oil, or a change in the level of world trade. These are of a different order of magnitude from a shift in demand from oranges to apples, or from one kind of orange to another. To a discernible degree they may change equilibrium real output and its composition, employment, and real wages. The task of basic macro-economics is to explain this. It is not helped by confusing it with general micro-economic equilibrium. The kind of considerations that suggest that the economy can find its way back from small deviations to an equilibrium path do not necessarily apply to large deviations.

Lastly, and reverting to methodology, fundamental theory tended to be very much theoretical or analytical in that it was not looking for quick answers based on econometric estimation. The role of the interest rate, for example, in generating enough investment to take up full employment saving is considered in the abstract, and persists in this literature separate from empirical studies of the interest elasticity of private investment. A similar point may be made about the real balance effect on private expenditure. This is not to say that fundamental theory does not have the ultimate intention of empirical relevance and application, but rather that it does not proceed prematurely to such things. Perhaps it would be correct to refer to fundamental macro-economics as the logic of economic enquiry.

I have referred to three types of macro-economics, (a) the simple theoretical model, (b) the econometric estimates, and (c) the fundamental theories. Many of the remarks I have made about them are critical, and I shall go on in the next chapter to subject them to even more critical scrutiny. None the less, I do not intend to reach the conclusion that all macro-economics up to the late 1960s was erroneous and worthless.

Quite the contrary: macro-economics in the three decades
after the publication of the *General Theory* is noteworthy for
a great many achievements. The income—expenditure approach
extended to include the government budget and the international trade multiplier remains a powerful mode of analysis
that has not been superseded. The quantity theory, emphasising the monetary aspects of inflation and in the guise of the
monetary theory of the balance of payments, is also a powerful procedure. Each of the two approaches has limitations,
especially when price and quantity variations occur simultaneously, but there is a vast range of issues for which they
come to the practically correct explanation, point to the
relevant data, and offer useful policy advice. Moreover,
econometric methods applied to either theoretical style have
yielded a vast array of estimates which at the least have the
negative merit of showing that almost all *simpliste* presup-
positions about the workings of the economic system are
doubtful. Whether they have helped very much on the positive
side, especially above the level of commonsense, is rather more
doubtful. But perhaps that is not the best way of judging it. If
we are unable to establish many, if any, permanent economic
laws, we have instead been able to establish a high-powered
permanent procedure for the investigation of quantitative
economic data. In other words, despite my strictures on the
failures of econometrists, econometrics remains a valuable part
of the armoury of the economist as critic, even though, like so
many other weapons, it can also fall into the hands of the
economist as terrorist.

My initial discussion of the old macro-economics was in the
simplest terms possible. This was largely for reasons of clarity
of exposition. It was also to enable me to make the point that
a great deal of allegedly more sophisticated theory is not,
from a methodological standpoint, more sophisticated at all.
This is especially true of Keynesian linear income—expenditure
models. Reverting to equation 1, if X is a vector of dependent

variables or outputs, A/P a vector of independent variables or inputs, and B a matrix, the system under discussion is *ipso facto* no more significant or complex. It is rather more burdensome from a data storage and manipulation point of view, but that is pretty trivial in the era of the large-scale computer, let alone the microprocessor. Thus there is nothing necessarily more interesting in a model that divides consumer expenditure or private investment into several categories, or has several equations for determining the balance of payments on current account rather than one, or disaggregates the money supply, or computes the wholesale price index as well as the retail price index and the gross domestic product deflator. Naturally enough, it is possible that forecasting may improve as a result of such disaggregation, and, obviously, if it is a particular category of consumer expenditure or foreign input that we need to forecast, we need to disaggregate accordingly. But this is *ad hoc* and has no special connection with fundamental theory at all.

There is a world of difference between a large model which is a blown-up and disaggregated version of a small model, and a large and more extensive theory as opposed to a smaller, narrower one. If, therefore, we concentrate on macro-economic theory especially in its Keynesian variants we note the following extensions:

1   A labour market in which both demand and supply curves are functions of the real wage, but in which relative money wages have a role to perform.
2   A money market in which, for given expectations of a largely financial kind, the money rate of interest equates the stock demand and supply of money for any level of income. Residually, a bond market (typically in public sector paper) is also brought into equilibrium.
3   A market for foreign exchange which in turn is related to goods markets in exports and imports. The goods

markets reach equilibrium, but in a world of fixed exchange rates governments intervene with sales and purchases of foreign and domestic currencies.

4   A government which raises direct and indirect taxes,
    makes transfer payments, and buys a share of final
    output, and employs a fraction of the labour force.

5   A division of markets into those where expenditure
    is largely a function of income, either total or disposable,
    and those where other variables — chiefly financial ones,
    such as the rate of interest, business and household
    liquidity, and real balances — have a major part to play.

The purpose of mentioning these extensions is twofold. Firstly,
they offer an agenda for analysis and empirical investigation.
Secondly, they enable me to reiterate the points of similarity
and differences at this level and at this stage of Keynesianism
and monetarism.

An example of the first is the labour market. No macro-
economic theory can regard itself as approaching completeness
without an account of the determination of real and money
wages. Detailed study of the labour market (or that class of
markets) must be high on the priority list of the applied
econometrist and the empirical researcher generally.[10]

A second example concerns the mix of direct and indirect
taxes.[11] In conventional income—expenditure theory it is
possible to show that, holding total tax revenue constant, a shift
from direct to indirect taxes is contractionary, i.e. it lowers
effective demand and real income. But, if there is no effect on
the government's budget position, the money supply in
nominal terms will be unaffected. If the relevant deflator
includes indirect taxes, the real money supply will fall. Thus
both the I—S and the L—M curve shift to the left, implying
that there is a monetary effect reinforcing the fiscal effect. In
these circumstances it cannot be said *a priori* what happens
to the rate of interest, which may rise (implying a crowding

out of private investment) or fall (implying a crowding in). Moreover, it is surely reasonable to argue that the labour supply function depends on real wages after tax. The question must be asked: if the tax mix affects consumer expenditure, will it not also affect the supply of labour? Lastly, if indirect taxes are not borne wholly by consumers (which the theory typically assumes they are), will the tax mix also not affect exports and imports? Will not an increase in indirect taxes encourage the former and discourage the latter?

These questions lead me straight back to doctrinal controversy. Before going on to much more complex issues, I would assert that there would not be a great deal of difference of substance between many Keynesians and monetarists in their approach to the issues under discussion, especially if emphasis is placed on the short term. Thus I am sure that both Keynesians and monetarists would recognise that, if the initial position were one of full employment, the contraction of effective demand at the going real wage rate (accomplished, say, by tax changes) would give rise to unemployment and something akin to a labour market disequilibrium. In addition, to the extent that both sides agreed that real balances appeared in the expenditure function of the private sector, and concentrating entirely on comparative statics, a new full employment equilibrium would exist at a lower nominal price and money wage level. (Apart from foreign trade effects the price level must fall by more than the percentage rise in indirect taxes. To fall only as much would restore real money balances to their opening level, but would do nothing to offset the leftward shift of the I–S curve.) Where they would start to differ is in answering the following sorts of questions:

1 Is it sensible to take full employment as the typical opening position?
2 Is it sensible to concentrate on comparative static comparisons of opening and closing positions?

3 Is it sensible to argue that the real disposable wage, and therefore labour supply, is not affected by the tax mix but that real expenditure is? The real wage net of tax is $W(1-t_1)/P(1+t_2)$, where W is the money wage, P the price level in factor cost terms, t_1 the rate of direct taxation, and t_2 the rate of indirect taxation. For practical purposes this may be approximated by $W(1-t)/P$, where $t = t_1 + t_2$. Is it satisfactory, therefore, to treat real consumption as a function of $Y(1-t)/P$ and also to ignore the fact that total tax revenue is equal to $t_1 Y + t_2 PC$, and treat it as equal to tY?

The answer to this last question is pretty straightforward. It is not unreasonable to approximate the consumption function in these terms, but it may be a mistake to aggregate the tax revenue function in the same way. The reason is simply that a switch from direct to indirect taxes involves revenue losses, so that a cut in the former implies a larger rise in the latter to maintain tax revenues. The result is then that total expenditure and national income will fall.

My conclusion from all this is that both pure fiscalism and pure monetarism, in so far as anyone believes in them at all, are mistaken. The monetary consequences even of a balanced budget change in fiscal structure need to be examined, and it is also important to see how the effect of a monetary change depends on the fiscal structure, i.e. on the tax mix.

These issues take us directly into policy and the public sector. One purpose of this book is to enquire into how macro-economics has changed over the years since Keynes's *General Theory* and the dominance of the Keynesians. A second and related purpose is to consider whether and to what extent the economy has changed.

In the past three decades the following changes seem most important:

1 The rise in the fraction of the labour force which is unionised.[12]

2 The rise in personal savings, personal wealth, and access by the household to sources of credit.
3 The rise in the fraction of the economy dominated by large firms, coupled with the growth of the multi-national enterprise.
4 The rise in the ratio of international to domestic trade.
5 The rise of international capital markets and the increased international mobility of capital.
6 The rise in the ratio of public expenditure to national income, of transfer incomes to total disposable incomes, and of the fraction of the labour force which works in the public sector.

Although only the last is specifically to do with economic policy, all these developments are relevant to policy. Some of them I discuss later in the context of the theory of expectations and especially the theory of rational expectations.

All I wish to do here is to point to some extremely important questions, which for the most part do not have satisfactory answers. Given these developments (and they cannot be gainsaid), how does macro-economics take cognisance of them? Is it that the broad theory remains the same, but the parameters change? If the answer to this question is yes (and many economists say it is), how can that be? Is it really true that the micro structure of the system is so irrelevant? If the answer is no, the theory itself must change, which leads to the question: what have been the basic changes in theory?

In the case of the propensity to consume, when national income is low most people will be poor enough to be income-constrained. Their net wealth will be zero, as will their access to any sizeable degree of credit. They will be paid cash on Friday and almost all that cash will be back in the bank by Monday at the latest. For these people the Keynesian consumption function (with a worker's propensity to save of zero) will be a correct hypothesis. In addition, since their holdings of cash will be equal to their money wage on one day and will be run down to zero in two more days, for them there will be no real balance effect. Essentially, money balances will be proportional to wages and prices, and real balances will be constant. In such an economy the real balance effect and the wealth effect can work only through capitalists who may already have a marginal propensity to consume of zero. It is difficult to see, therefore, why raising their real balances will cause them to spend more in a way that is particularly expansionary.

It is easy to appreciate that, as the economy develops, and especially as an increasing fraction of households have positive wealth, real cash balances and access to credit, consumption will be less constrained and determined by current real income. A wealth effect and a permanent income theory may become relevant where once they were irrelevant.

Similar kinds of points could be made about other changes, and I do not pursue them, solely for reasons of lack of space. Instead I wish to concentrate on the significance of the rise of the public sector.[13]

In the standard economic model, two key variables are total public expenditure on goods and services (sometimes subdivided into capital and current), total taxes (sometimes subdivided into direct and indirect) and total transfer payments. The aggregate goods market equilibrium is then given as: total expenditure $(I+C+G+X)$ equals total supply $(Y+M)$ or total domestic expenditure $(I+C+G+X-M)$ equals total domestic output (Y). (Within this, balance of trade equilibrium might be defined as the value of exports plus transfer payments from abroad equalling the value of imports plus transfer payments made to foreigners.) Labour market equilibrium occurs when the total demand for labour equals the supply. This amount of employment is then what determines national output.

This model is useful for some purposes. If, however, employment in the public sector is of significant size, a different model is needed. The reason is twofold. One is that labour market equilibrium is affected by the government's demand for employees. The second is that goods market equilibrium needs to be expressed as the equation of the supply of private sector output with the demand.

The essential point is easy to make. Imagine an economy in full equilibrium. Suppose now that the government endeavours to recruit more workers. It may raise the real wage (assuming the supply of labour is upward-sloping), causing a reduction in private sector employment, although not in total employment. Private sector output will fall, because fewer workers are employed in the private sector at the higher real wage. Total demand for private sector output will probably rise as total wage income rises as a result of both an increase in the number of people employed and the real wage they are paid. The restoration of equilibrium requires either an increase in taxes or a reduction in public sector purchases of private sector output. If the tax rate is given, the maintenance of equilibrium imposes a choice or trade-off between the two kinds of public expenditure.

It can be shown that (making the usual assumptions on the likely slopes of various spending or supply functions), with given taxes, an increase of public sector employment offset by a reduction of public expenditure on private sector output to maintain equilibrium, (a) leads to an increase in total employment, i.e. it is employment-creating, (b) leads to an increase in total real public expenditure. In general, of its three instruments – the tax rate, public sector employment, and public sector purchases of private sector output – only two are at the government's disposal, the third being determined by the need to maintain full employment equilibrium. If the condition of a balanced budget (or a fixed deficit) is added, there is a further constraint on the government, enabling it to choose freely only one instrument.

An analysis of this kind is of value for three reasons:

1   It clarifies the position of the public sector at full
     employment.
2   It separates the equilibrium position of the public sector
     from its stabilising role.[14]
3   It indicates how the public sector may be the source of a
     disequilibrium in the real economy.

The last of these is not a negligible possibility. Thus, relevant
to present conditions, excessive public sector employment
may lead to too low a level of private sector employment to
generate output equal to private sector final demands, public
sector final demands, and, in an open economy, exports. To
be contrasted with our earlier analysis, the increase in public
sector employment may crowd out employment in the tradable
sector, worsening the balance of payments from the supply
side, so to speak.

Another possibility worth exploring is that disequilibrium
may be created by the government as employer being the
settler of real wages, firstly in the public sector and then in
the economy at large. Suppose, other things being equal,
that the government raises the real wages it pays in equilibrium.[15] Its impact effect is both to unbalance the budget
(involving a possible rise in the money supply) and to create an
excess demand for private sector output. The private sector
will not find it profitable to meet this demand, which will
then spill over into imports, or give rise directly to price
increases. It may also stimulate workers in the private sector
to press for higher real wages themselves. To the extent that
they succeed the private sector demand for labour will be
reduced, together with private sector output. The excess
demand for this output may be intensified, and the balance of
payments position worsened. The outcome may thus be
inflation, rising unemployment and a worsening of the
balance of payments, all attributable to faulty government
policy.

Notes

[1] In saying this I am not trying to suggest that we are dealing here with two homogenous groups. As far as the monetarists are concerned, there have been several statements of their credo. In *Money and the Economy. A Monetarist View* (Addison-Wesley, 1978) W. Poole offers us eight articles of faith. T. Mayer offers as many as twelve in 'Monetarism: economic analysis or Weltanschauung?' (*Banca Nazionale de Lavoro Quarterly Review,* September 1978). The Keynesians have not gone in for such lists of propositions, although one could be inferred, for example, from *The General Theory and After.* Part II, *Defence and Development. The Collected Writings of J. M. Keynes,* ed. D. Moggridge (Macmillan, 1973).

[2] Thus Poole tells us, 'It is technically feasible to control the money stock and, therefore, the government should be held responsible for the consequences of monetary instability' (*ibid.,* p. 2). It is also worth recalling an early remark of Keynes. He had for long been associated with Liberal Party expansionary policies of public expenditure and public works to deal with unemployment, but he had this to say as well: 'Naturally I am interested not only in the diagnosis, but also in the cure; and many pages of my book are devoted to the latter. But I consider my suggestions for a cure, which, avowedly, are not worked out completely, are on a different plane from the diagnosis. They are not meant to be definitive; they are subject to all sorts of special assumptions and are necessarily related to the particular conditions of the time.' ('The General Theory of Employment', *Quarterly Journal of Economics,* February 1937, reprinted in Moggridge, *op. cit.,* p. 122.)

[3] That would certainly be a fair comment on much of the more technical parts of my own *Theory of Macroeconomic Policy* (Philip Allan, 1973).

[4] One of the more remarkable things to emerge from the Royal Economic Society's collected editions of the Keynes material is the wide ambiguity as to what the classical theory of employment was supposed to be. The interchanges with Hawtrey and Pigou on the classical labour supply curve are quite extraordinary (Moggridge, *op. cit., passim*). I must add that I am coming to the conclusion that Keynes not

only invented the Keynes theory but was also the originator of the classical theory. It is also my view that the Friedman versions of monetarism are also Keynesian in a different form and with a change in terminology. It is important to mention in connection with all this the major essay by B. Corry, 'Keynes in the history of economic thought: some reflections' (in *Keynes and Laissez-faire,* ed. A. Thirlwall, Macmillan, 1978). We do disagree, however, in the relative importance we attach to Keynes and the classics. It seems to me that Corry is right that Keynes was grossly unfair to many of the economists he criticised, notably Pigou — about as unfair as the protagonists of the neo-classical synthesis are to Keynes! Incidentally, in this connection there is one of Keynes's remarks that should never be neglected: 'Our criticism of the accepted classical theory of economics has consisted not so much in finding logical flaws in its analysis as in pointing out that its tacit assumptions are seldom or never satisfied, with the result that it cannot solve the economic problems of the actual world. But if our central controls succeed in establishing an aggregate volume of output corresponding to full employment as nearly as is practicable, the classical theory comes into its own again from this point onwards.' (*The General Theory of Employment, Interest and Money,* Macmillan, 1936, p. 378.) It is of interest to discuss the question of how original monetarism really is. Consider Dennis Robertson's 'A survey of modern monetary controversy' (*The Manchester School,* 1938) or 'Creeping inflation' (*Bulletin of the London and Cambridge Economic Service,* 1955). There is not a lot that we are offered by more recent writers that is missing from those essays. For example, '. . . the planned orderly fall in the value of money would be in danger of turning into a landslide, generating not a comfortable condition of "full employment" but a hectic and disorderly muddle, which could only be checked, at the cost of much disemployment and distress, by the re-establishment of drastic monetary disciplines' (*op. cit.,* p. 253, in Sir Dennis Robertson, *Essays in Money and Interest,* ed. Sir John Hicks, Fontana, 1966). I would also draw attention to Gunnar Myrdal's *Monetary Equilibrium,* which appeared in English in 1939 but was originally published in Sweden eight years earlier. Myrdal and the other great Swedish economists are usually discussed as precursors of Keynes, but this book is extraordinarily monetarist in flavour. It consists partly in the emphasis on price levels (employment and output not changing much), and on the distinction between what is real and what is nominal in the interest rate. But much more exciting is the emphasis on expectations or anticipations, and the dynamics that result therefrom.

[5] May I add a word on large econometric models, which now have a life of their own. It is of interest to ask of each of them, what is its macro-economic theoretical foundation? Of the four major models with which I am acquainted, I think I can answer this question in two cases, Cambridge and the London Business School, and not answer it in two others, the National Institute and the Treasury. This does not mean that the latter are inferior models, and certainly their proponents claim as much success in forecasting as anybody. What I am saying is that on the face of it they do not make sense, and it would be a worthwhile task to study them (as others of us study the economy itself) with a view to explaining their behaviour. A useful reference in this connection is *Demand Management,* ed. M. Posner, Heinemann, 1978.

[6] Sir John Hicks has been at great pains to emphasise this in many of his writings of recent times. See in particular his preface to *Economic Perspectives* (Oxford University Press, 1977). He also refers back to his criticism of the temporary equilibrium method in *Capital and Growth* (Oxford University Press, 1965). '. . . the artificiality of such constructions is only too obvious. They do deliberate violence to the *order* in which in the real world (in *any* real world) events occur' (p. 73).

[7] M. Peston, 'The microeconomics of the Phillips curve', in H. G. Johnson and A. R. Nobay, *The Current Inflation,* (Macmillan, 1971), p. 126.

[8] There is a fascinating comment by Ohlin: 'In this [i.e. perfect competition] as in some other respects Keynes does not seem to have been radical enough in freeing himself from the conventional assumption. When reading his book one sometimes wonders whether he never discussed imperfect competition with Mrs Robinson.'(Moggridge, *op. cit.,* p. 196.) Keynes replied, 'I have not been able to make out here what you are driving at. The reference to imperfect competition is very perplexing. I cannot see how on earth it comes in. Mrs Robinson, I may mention, read my proofs without discovering

any connection.' (*Ibid.*, p. 180.) If I may recall Mrs Robinson's famous remark on Keynes not understanding the General Theory, for once she too missed an essential point!

[9] This kind of consideration lies at the heart of Axel Leijohufvud's masterpiece, *On Keynesian Economics and the Economics of Keynes* (Oxford University Press, 1968). While one may agree with much that is contained in that book, the distinction he makes between Keynes and the Keynesians is surely rather exaggerated, if not actually mistaken. Although a valid distinction can be made between (a) fundamental theory, and the fundamental problem of a self-stabilising system, (b) the I—S/L—M type theory, and (c) elementary income and expenditure models, the evidence is that Keynes was sympathetic to all three, and used them according to the purpose in mind. This is especially apparent if we examine *Activities, 1939–1945. International War Finance. The Collected Writings of John Maynard Keynes,* vol. XXII (ed. D. Moggridge, Macmillan, 1978). This volume is full of material of a Keynesian kind. It is also apparent from Keynes's analysis of how we were to pay for the war that he was aware of the P.S.B.R., and of the connection between the external deficit and the internal financial problem. Finally, his discussion of subsidies, indirect taxation and the cost of living is as contemporary as anything written in the Department of Prices from 1974 to 1978.

[10] Concerning the labour market, we know a great many little things, but need to know one big thing. We are all foxes and need a hedgehog.

[11] M. H. Peston, 'The tax mix and effective demand', *Public Finance,* No. 3, 1971. The argument that follows points to the incompleteness of the analysis in this article.

[12] In the mid-1930s about 25 per cent of the U.K. labour force was in trade unions. The proportion is now 52 per cent. Moreover, some 85 per cent of workers in the public sector are in trade unions. Of course, there is more to it that that, since the percentage of the labour force unionised was high in the 1920s as well.

[13] The argument that follows is in the spirit of the theoretical analysis of R. Bacon and W. Eltis, *Britain's Economic Problem. Too Few Producers* (Macmillan, 1976). My emphasis is different from theirs, and I am much less

critical of the public sector than they are.

[14] This analysis can be generalised to show that the problem of policy away from full employment is more complicated than is commonly realised. In particular, it is possible to prove that the same combination of private sector output and employment can arise from Keynesian deficient demand or classical excessive real wages. In the former case a marginal increase of public sector employment raises private sector output and employment, but in the latter case it merely adds to effective demand.

[15] Of course, it does this by paying higher money wages relative to the given level of prices ruling at any time.

Chapter Two

Chapter I was concerned in large part with Keynesian economics in a variety of forms, including those which have a distinctly classical and monetarist flavour. My concern was to emphasise the strengths and weaknesses of that kind of economics both as theory and as an applied discipline. The purpose of this chapter is to extend my earlier critical remarks and also to begin to consider some more recent contributions to macro-economics. Some of these are natural extensions of what went before; others represent a rather more distinct break with earlier thinking. Of the former, let me reply to one criticism before I proceed further. It can be said of many of the extensions I am about to scrutinise that they are more a matter of change of emphasis than anything more drastic. With this I readily agree, but am bound to add that the replacement of an incorrect emphasis by a correct one can be pretty important. After all, what are simple Keynesian models but simple classical models with the greater emphasis being placed on quantity rather than price adjustment?[1]

The first extension of theory concerns the role of constraints. In Keynes's *General Theory* consumption is determined by income to a very considerable extent because the latter constrains the former. The poor household has no liquid or marketable assets and can hardly borrow. It can only spend its income. But, more generally, there appears to be a financing requirement for all sectors of the economy. From a negative standpoint, an excess of expenditure over income must be financed by running down cash balances, or by borrowing short or long-term. From a positive standpoint, an excess of income over expenditure must be disposed of by acquiring cash balances or lending short or long-term. This is true of the household sector, the non-financial business sector, the financial sector, the foreign trade sector, and the government sector.[2]

I was tempted initially to argue that the key breakthrough in thought was the introduction of the government budget constraint, with its counterpart, the public sector borrowing requirement. But this is nonsense. There is a budget constraint for each and every sector and a borrowing or lending requirement. Of course, this is not to say that the financial debts of all sectors are equivalent, but it is to insist that it is an important theoretical task to explain why some debts are treated generally as money and others are not. *A priori* it is obviously possible that some private sector non-bank debt or overseas debt could be treated as money (high-powered or otherwise). It is also obviously possible that interest-bearing government debt could be treated as money.

Having made that point, however, it does seem to me that the consideration of these constraints, and especially the government budget constraint, were seriously neglected until some dozen years ago.[3] They are now recognised as of overwhelming importance, and bringing them explicitly into the analysis improves various simple models beyond all recognition. This is true both of quantity adjustment and of price adjustment models.

Concentrating on the closed economy, to start with, we have the condition $I-S+G-T=0$. On the usual assumption that S exceeds I, this means that the net lending requirement of the private sector must equal the borrowing requirement of the government. If the government borrowing requirement is divided in a predetermined way between the issue of high-powered money and other borrowing of various maturities, the financial system must adjust so as to provide the household and non-bank private sectors with whatever money and bonds it wishes. Given the rate of interest, the government must adjust the high-powered money part of its borrowing requirement to meet the public's demand for money. Alternatively, given the government's supply of high-powered money, the rate of interest must be allowed to adjust to equate the resulting supply of money with the demand.

Curiously enough, this has always been well known to practical men (including Keynes) and is vital to liquidity preference theory, yet it was neglected in constraint terms for so long. The neglect is doubly curious when it is realised that here lies the fundamental connection between fiscal and financial (or monetary) policy. All those past debates about the independent use of taxation and money supply as instruments are seen to be rather silly once the private sector lending requirement or the public sector borrowing requirement is made explicit.[4] An increase in public spending not only has income effects, it also has public sector and private sector financial effects. The extra private sector saving so generated must be held in some paper asset form. The extra public sector borrowing requirement must provide those paper assets. Which assets are issued and the attitudes to them influence the money and bond supply and the rate of interest, and thus in due course the flow of income and the level of prices of goods.

Two other consequences of this approach need to be noted. One is that the so-called helicopter money experiment of the naive monetarists is irrelevant to serious analysis almost to the point of being misleading. The second is that it is permissible and may be interesting to start from the private sector lending requirement and see what this imposes on the public sector, rather than always to proceed in the reverse direction. An increase in the private sector propensity to save which would generate a higher private sector surplus must be met, if equilibrium is to be maintained, by an increase in the public sector borrowing requirement. Moreover, if within that extra saving there is a greater demand for money at the prevailing rate of interest, the government must supply (or cause to be supplied) some extra money if the interest rate is not to rise. As far as first principles are concerned, the change in the money stock is just as capable of being part of a response mechanism as it is of being an initiating cause.

The second extension of the theory is to do with the distinction between stocks and flows. It is probably incorrect to refer to this as an extension, since it is much more a return to some of the debates that followed immediately on the publication of Keynes's *General Theory*. In that theory the distinction between stocks and flows is fundamental, and it is also fundamental to the critics of Keynes.

The chief flows are, of course, income and its constituents. The chief stocks are money and bonds. Some of the flows add to stocks. Investment is the increase in real capital. Private saving is the addition to the wealth of the private sector. The difference between government spending and taxation is a flow of high-powered money and government bonds to the private sector which adds to the sector's stock of those things. The difference between export and import flows, together with net current grants (or transfer payments) overseas, involves a change in the composition of U.K. holdings of foreign assets or foreign holdings of U.K. assets.

Now, as I have said, far from all this being new, it is old stuff for the macro-economics of the 1930s and '40s. It is what Robertson and Keynes were arguing about.[5] Once again, what has changed is the emphasis. Whereas the theory used to concentrate on goods and money market equilibrium in the short term — a state of affairs best illustrated by the I–S/L–M apparatus — it is now seen to be necessary to pay more attention to the sequence of such temporary equilibria. The three obvious examples are:

1   The Blinder—Solow analysis of the government financing
     requirement and the consequences of all that,[6]
2   The domestic monetary ramifications of changes in foreign
     reserves due to the state of the balance of payments,[7]
3   The growth of private wealth and its influence on
     expenditure, and the growth of real capital and its
     influence on productive capacity.

All these illustrate the point that short-period equilibrium
really is temporary. Even if nothing else changes, expenditure
plans next period will differ from this because households
and firms have more nominal wealth or are more liquid. Goods
market equilibrium next period may require a higher level of
effective demand because of the growth of capacity. Labour
market equilibrium next period may require a higher real
wage because of a rising marginal productivity of labour.

None of this in itself is difficult to cope with, but pro-
ceeding from temporary to what may be called full or final
equilibrium can yield some rather interesting results. Thus
the theorem that relates an increase in government expenditure
to the ultimate increase in output via the expansion of the
money supply is a kind of balanced budget result which
earlier theorists had overlooked. They had concentrated on a
balanced budget temporary equilibrium. What we have now is
a balanced budget terminal equilibrium. What is important
about this result is threefold:

1   That there is a final equilibrium, although it may not be a
     stable one.
2   That the expansionary power of extra government
     expenditure is so much larger in the long term than in the
     short.
3   That this expansionary power derives from the monetary
     consequences of the initial expenditure.

(There is also a fourth consequence relating to this which
concerns its effect on expectations. I deal with that later on.)

A similar conclusion can be derived about the expansionary effects of exports. Starting from balance of payments equilibrium, a rise in exports leads to a reverse inflow which, if allowed to be fully reflected in a rise in the money supply, leads to increasing imports until balance of payments equilibrium is eventually restored. Here, too, we have the analogous theorem that the rise in income will in the final equilibrium be much larger than in the temporary equilibrium, and that the multiplier will be the inverse of the marginal propensity to import. This too happens via an expansion of the domestic money stock.

The analogy can be taken further by noting that, just as a bond-financed public sector deficit generates interest payments and, therefore, a potentially larger deficit in subsequent periods, so a foreign-borrowing-financed balance of payments deficit leads to a larger deficit on the invisible account in later periods.

The two models can, as is now well known, be put together. If both taxes and imports are income-related, the multiplier from an export expansion will be $1/(t+m)$, where t is the effective marginal tax rate and m the marginal propensity to import. Equilibrium will now be achieved with a permanent balance of payments surplus counterbalanced by a permanent budget surplus (assuming that the initial point was one of balance on both accounts). The excess money inflow can be just offset by the excess tax payments. In other words, a negative domestic credit expansion (DCE) will offset a positive rise in the reserves. (I ignore whether in a broader sense this can be regarded as a true final equilibrium.) Thus, to consider another variation, the monetary effects of an expansion in public expenditure will cause a larger rise in national income and a greater worsening of the current balance of payments than is suggested by the usual multiplier model.

In the final equilibrium, with no increase in the money supply or net expansion of government bonds, private sector saving equals private sector investment, i.e. there is no net acquisition of financial assets by the private sector. This is to be compared with the 'New Cambridge' theory, which takes the rate of acquisition of net financial assets by the private sector as given.[8] There too, therefore, an increase in public expenditure cannot lead to an increase in the rate of acquisition of financial assets by the private sector. It must instead show up in a full balance of payments offset. Moreover, if imports and taxes are income-related, the New Cambridge multiplier must equal the final equilibrium multiplier of a Blinder-Solow model.

My third point of departure is the natural rate of unemployment and the concept of full employment. In both Keynesian and classical models full employment is defined relative to an aggregate demand for labour as a function of the real wage paid by employers and an aggregate supply of labour as a function of the real wage received by employees. The two real wages are not the same. The first should be interpreted as the average cost of hiring a given number of units of labour, and the latter the real receipts of those units. Implicit in the analysis too are such relative prices as wage costs relative to other factor costs, and receipts from work relative to receipts from non-work. Beyond all that, since both the demand and the supply curves are aggregates and abstractions, they hide a great deal that is going on at the micro-economic level. In the vicinity of their intersection we can extend the demand curve to allow for a quantity of normal vacancies corresponding to the normal minor changes in individual firms' demand for labour, and extend the supply curve to allow for workers en route from one job to another. In other words, the intersection of the aggregate supply and demand curves for labour is compatible with minor firm and household disequilibria in which some vacancies and some unemployment persist. Moreover, depending on the law and the way it is administered, the registered unemployed will include workers who claim to be available for work, but who will avoid as long as possible taking employment at current real wages and conditions.

Taking various institutional and policy factors as given, full employment may be defined as that level of employment corresponding to the equilibrium real wage. And there is no difficulty for either a Keynesian or classical economist in accepting a modicum of unemployment as compatible with full employment.[9] Beyond that there may be more unemployment and less employment either as the market fails to equilibrate of its own accord or because of some external disequilibrating factor. It is said, for example, that the classical view of the causes of unemployment was that the real wage differed from the equilibrium one. If the real wage were too high, employers would be willing to hire less labour than the full-employment quantity. If the real wage were too low, fewer workers than the full-employment numbers would be forthcoming.

Now, without denying the classical view that an incorrect real wage may be the cause of unemployment on occasions, it is hard to see that in itself as a cause of cyclical variations in employment and unemployment. Of course, a rise in money wages without an equivalent rise in prices, or more likely a fall in prices without an equivalent fall in money wages, may lead to lay-offs and unemployment. But surely that is likely to be of the chronic, stagnation kind rather than the cyclical kind?

Cyclical employment is surely likely to be the result of some external cyclical force such as effective demand. There may then be real wage consequences, and these may add chronic stagnation to the cycle, but they will be consequences rather than initiating causes. In other words, even classical unemployment is most probably the result of Keynesian causes.

Whatever the view that one takes of this, however, the classical and Keynesian theorists both saw full employment as a *maximum* and the unemployment at full employment as a minimum.[10] Employment fluctuated in a range below this maximum, while unemployment fluctuated in a range above this minimum. The average level of employment (about which employment appeared to fluctuate) was less than full employment. The average level of unemployment (about which unemployment appeared to fluctuate) was greater than at full employment.

This view is to be contrasted with more recent discussions of such phenomena as the natural rate of unemployment in two ways. Firstly, some theorists appear to see the economic fluctuations and the natural rate of unemployment as depending on wage and price expectations on the part of buyers and sellers of labour. Secondly, some of those theorists *define* the natural rate of unemployment in a logically quite different way, namely to say that it is the rate compatible with a stable inflation rate.

Before considering both these points it is worth recalling Friedman's direct definition of the natural rate.

At any moment of time there is some level of unemployment that is consistent with equilibrium in the structure of *real* wage rates. At that level of unemployment, real wages are tending on the average to rise at a 'normal' secular rate, i.e. at a rate that can be indefinitely maintained so long as capital formation, technological improvements, etc., remain on their long term trends ... The 'natural rate of unemployment', in other words, is the level that would be ground out by the Walrasian system of general equilibrium equations, provided there is imbedded in them the actual structural characteristics of the labour and commodity markets, including market imperfections, stochastic variability in demand and supplies, the costs of gathering information about job vacancies and labour vacancies, the costs of mobility, and so on.[11]

This is what might be called a natural extension of the concept of full employment as conceived by Keynes and the classics. The trouble with it is that as a generalisation it begs far too many questions and seems to combine both the trivial and the potentially self-contradictory. If *every* structural characteristic of the labour market is included, it is hard to see why all states of the economy are not ones of full employment. Presumably Friedman has in mind a method of distinguishing what is truly structural from all the other forces determining what happens in the labour market. But, if he has, he has not enlightened us on the matter, and nor have his colleagues. He himself states, 'One problem is that [we] cannot know what the "natural rate" is. Unfortunately, we have as yet devised no method to estimate accurately and readily the natural rate of either interest or unemployment. And the natural rate will itself change from time to time.'[12] To ask the most obvious question of all, is one of the relevant givens past experience of fluctuations in the economy and its levels of unemployment, and consequential expectations of future fluctuations? If it is, there are logical difficulties to overcome concerning what the Walrasian general equilibrium equations grind out. If it is not, the question is simply begged as far as the existence of and nature of the relevant general equilibrium are concerned.

The more apparent difficulty is in the emphasis on *real* wage rates. These are certainly emphasised in the more elementary model of the labour market we have discussed. But once we generalise to encompass 'actuality', nothing can be taken for granted. The structure of labour markets must include the bargaining propensities and powers of both sides of industry, together with such powerful institutional forces as norms, including what is regarded as the normal rate of increase in real wages, and normal relativities. It cannot be assumed *a priori* that these structural and institutional forces will or could grind out a Walrasian solution in real wages and employment in the sense of a unique equilibrium, other than in a trivial sense that if two levels of unemployment are consistent with the same level and rate of change of real wages there must be some cause which gives rise to one rather than the other.[13]

My own view is that much of the discussion on the natural rate of unemployment is based on misconception. It must surely be the case for an enormously wide range of institutional structures (I am tempted to say independent of institutional structure) that the — largely given in the short and medium term — underlying rate of growth of real output will be the chief determinant of the growth of real wages. In addition, again virtually independent of the structural characteristics of the labour and commodity markets, an increase in the level of real wages must have a tendency to lower the demand for labour. In other words, the demand curve for labour will for the most part vary inversely with the real wage paid, and will move outwards at a rate close to if not equal to the rate of growth of productive capacity. To the extent, therefore, that the desire for employment is determined by the real wage received, it is possible to conceive of full employment and the real wage being broadly determined together in a kind of equilibrium. It will also be the case that a lower level of employment will go hand in hand with a higher real wage paid, but not with a higher rate of growth of the real wage (except in the transitional phase).[14]

If we then enquire about a possible relationship between unemployment and the money wage, it is easy to see both a temporary and a steady-state connection. Let us begin with the latter at the point of full employment labour market equilibrium. It is generally recognised that in such a state all markets are buoyant, real incomes in a cyclical economy are unusually high, and decision-makers (not excluding the government) will be biased in an optimistic direction. Thus, although the system is in equilibrium, its bias will be towards excess demand, rising prices and rising money wages.[15] Typically, real growth will appear as increasing nominal factor incomes at given prices or, even more likely, increasing nominal incomes at rising prices. It will not be usual for nominal incomes to be fixed and prices to fall.[16] Thus full employment will generally be an inflationary state of affairs, but not intrinsically an explosive one.

Fiscal and monetary policy will be adjusted to allow this, for the obvious reason that more stringent attempts to keep price levels constant will lead to real losses both in terms of industrial conflict and in terms of sustained periods of unemployment.

At effective demand levels below, but not greatly below, those necessary for full employment there will be rather less buoyancy of markets, and less upward bias in goods and factor prices.

Imagine now a lower level of effective demand but one that is maintained. Both the Keynesian and the classical analyses of the labour market, applied realistically, would lead to the view that at employment levels below full employment money wages and prices would rise more slowly than at full employment. Both would tend to see the possibly new given level of real wages, once reached, being maintained by money wages rising at the same rate as prices, and a growing level of real wages being achieved by money wages rising faster than prices. Lower effective demand and higher unemployment would, if the new level and rate of growth of real wages were to remain undisturbed, be reached by moderating the rate of increase of money wages and prices. (There might also be a further effect if the lower employment level led to a higher than full employment level of real wages corresponding to a move along the labour demand curve.) There would not be much difficulty in both agreeing that the larger the unemployment level the more the rise of money wages would be moderated.

Where they would differ would be in whether the change in money wages might become negative. Even this, however, is not fundamental, since the General Theory did not entirely rule out wage cuts, and many classical economists (certainly including Pigou) recognised the downward stickiness of money wages.[17]

The chief difference between the two concerned the maintenance of effective demand at less than full employment levels through time. Essentially, the classics argued that a given rate of diminution of money wage increases (or money wage cuts) would lower real wages, if necessary, and stimulate effective demand so that full employment was restored. Thus the relationship between $\dot{W}$ and U was a transitory one. Either U would eventually fall or $\dot{W}$ would.

For the Keynesians the position was that the lowering of $\dot{W}$ as unemployment rose to a higher level was not an equilibrating process. The level of U could persist virtually indefinitely. Secondly, while accepting an attenuation of $\dot{W}$ for larger U, they did not see an acceleration in the decline of $\dot{W}$ if U persisted. (In both cases they might have added the proviso 'except in the long run', but would not have meant by this what the classics did. For the Keynesians that length of long run was irrelevant, i.e. it was longer than the life expectancy of anyone alive at the time. For the classics it was a period short enough to be of practical significance.)[18]

Note that the Keynesian view giving rise to a Phillips curve does not depend on money illusion. It is simply a characteristic of the system that excess supply in the labour market is regarded as not necessarily leading to real wage cuts or money wage cuts. And, even if it did, this would not be an especially efficacious method of restoring full employment.

On the question of whether the moderation in the rate of increase of money wages stays constant or intensifies, essentially the argument underlying the Phillips curve is that the higher level of unemployment leads to a fixed reduction in the rate of increase of money wages. The counter-argument is that in the longer run, if that given degree of moderation of wage pressure does not bring the unemployed back into employment, wage pressure will be moderated even more.

Reflecting on the two possibilities, it does seem reasonable to argue that restricting employment below full employment will lead to a deceleration in the rate of increase of money wages rather than a once-and-for-all shift. If, moreover, the government refuses to allow full employment to be restored, eventually the rate of increase of money wages will fall to some kind of institutional minimum. In other words, for employment levels below full employment, if enough time is allowed to pass, the slope of the Phillips curve would get flatter and flatter. Except in the neighbourhood of full employment, there will be little or no long-run trade-off. But, except in the very long run, which is surely not of practical relevance nor reflected in estimated Phillips curves, all that may be ignored.[19]

All this discussion has been based on the concept of full employment as a maximum. Can we go beyond that maximum, other than by institutional or structural change? Here the answer is surely quite clear-cut. If effective demand rises above the full-employment level of output, to the extent that attempts are made to meet this by expanding home production (rather than by importing more), employment may rise. But, if the demand and supply curves for labour have been defined correctly, this can only be a temporary phenomenon, although temporary could be a more than trivial interval of real time.

The way markets work, the excess demand will be met in the first instance by running down stocks, or by operating services at a higher level. Firms will be tempted to take on more labour at the going wage rate, but this will only be profitable if prices can be raised. They may raise prices so that the level of, and scale of increase in, real wages are reduced. In due course, however, workers will demand the restoration of the equilibrium real wage or reduce the supply of labour.[20]

It seems fairly certain, therefore, that an attempt to run the economy at a higher than full employment level must fail in a long run which is not of irrelevant length. Either inflation will accelerate (if monetary and fiscal policy permits), or there will be a gradual restoration of full employment (probably along a cyclical path).

What is not obvious, however, is why anyone should bother to any great extent with this case. There is nothing in Keynes's *General Theory* to suggest that he was an advocate of running the economy beyond the point of full employment. Equally, Keynesian theory has been about the maintenance of full employment, nor over-full employment.[21] The Phillips curve may have points on it above the full employment level, but no one has argued that these were sustainable indefinitely. The real issue was the more difficult one of determining what the full employment point was.

The concept of full employment, although of vital importance to macro-economics, is difficult to apply. It has been argued that the economy is in a condition of full employment when real wages are 'rising at a rate equal to the rate of productivity growth'. This is not satisfactory for two reasons. One is that Keynesian economics indicates that over a time period which may be extremely long real wages can grow at the rate of productivity growth while leaving a constant but sizeable level of unemployment. The second is that the *level* of real wages corresponding to full employment will change with the underlying structure of the economy. It is absurd to argue that when this happens full employment no longer exists. More to the point, the divergence of real wage growth from the underlying rate may be due either to a change in institutional structure or to a shift away from full employment. Except in the long period, and without other evidence, it is impossible to say which is which.

All this has led to a second definition of full employment (or the natural rate of unemployment), namely that it is the state of affairs which is compatible with a stable rate of inflation. This too runs into the difficulty that, in the

Keynesian view of the economy, in any reasonable time period (i.e. a period long relative to other factors changing) there will be a whole range of unemployment rates compatible with stable inflation. Even in a classical analysis as generalised by Friedman it is possible that the underlying rate of growth of the economy varies with the unemployment rate. In this case it is possible that there is more than one unemployment rate compatible with zero or stable inflation. There may be a low level of unemployment at which workers' demands for a high level of real wage growth can be met by a higher underlying rate of growth capacity. As unemployment increases, both the workers' demands and the economy's ability to meet them fall. It is then possible that there will be a high unemployment rate at which the two are equalised. Once this single possibility is recognised, multiple equilibrium can easily be established.

The argument is reinforced further when the bargaining nature of the labour market is considered explicitly. The existence of conflict over the distribution of real income can hardly be denied, and must be included in the definition of the natural rate of unemployment. If this is so, however, it again follows easily either that the economy may have no non-inflationary or stable inflationary equilibrium or it may have many.

For simplicity consider an economy in which the underlying growth rate is given. The problem is then the division of a predetermined cake. Let the conflict in these circumstances be of the sort usually known as the battle of the sexes game.[22] This means that, if a solution can be agreed, the whole cake is to be divided, but, if a solution cannot be agreed, only a smaller cake is shared. Within existing economic theory there is no proof that a determinate solution exists to such a game. All that can be said is that sometimes there is agreement and sometimes not, and all this depends on some nebulous notion of bargaining power. The important point in the present context is the simple one that there is nothing predetermined about the outcome of this bargaining situation. This year's division of the cake may differ from next year's, and neither or both may be correctly characterised as full employment or stable inflation.

We may then add a third player, namely the government. In any year in which the players come to an agreed solution, the government may adjust its policy to ensure that the agreement is realised. Where the solution is not agreed, the government may conciliate or it may adjust policy relative to the conflict. For example, if workers succeed in gaining a larger money wage increase than the underlying growth of capacity, the government may adopt a tight stance allowing the real increase but leading to unemployment and a decline in capacity utilisation. Alternatively, it may adopt a loose stance sabotaging the real increase by allowing prices to rise but maintaining full employment.

It cannot be assumed that this system does or can settle down into a single state. More likely it will experience a sequence of states, and no particular condition of the labour market at any one time will be associated with a stable or unstable inflation rate. To search for such a single natural unemployment rate is to search for a chimera. To argue that every time the inflation rate accelerates the natural unemployment rate has changed is to trivialise the whole analysis.

The conclusion from all this is not that full employment is a useless concept, or that inflation cannot result from attempts to run the economy at too high a rate of capacity utilisation. It can also be agreed that the highest degree of capacity utilisation or maximum growth rate can change. The important thing is not to analyse these matters in a mechanical way or to jump to conclusions *a priori* which cannot be tested by evidence independent of the hypothesis under examination. In particular, hypotheses dependent on employers' or employees' attitudes, expectations, perceptions of reality, bargaining power, etc., are always in danger of being tautological, arising *ex post facto* rather than *ex ante,* and are extremely difficult to test or subject to critical scrutiny.

Having said that, I must now go on in Chapter III to discuss recent developments in the analysis of expectations. The old macro-economics placed considerable weight on expectations. This was true of Swedish theory as well as Keynesian theory. The Austrian school, too, took expectations seriously.[23] The trouble was that expectations were *ad hoc,* and plucked from outside the model, so to speak. In some cases it seems difficult to do better than that, at least within the confines of economics. But it must be said that recent attempts to provide an economic theory of expectations represent a most exciting advance in economic theory.

Notes

[1] I do not wish this point to be taken quite literally. Rather, what I have in mind is Leijonhufvud's interpretation of Keynes as changing the Marshallian assumption on the relative elasticity of prices and output in the short run. (*Ibid.,* p. 37.)

[2] The correct specification of the *ex ante* constraint for a decision-maker is extremely difficult, and, in my opinion, has been insufficiently explored. The problem is multifold: (a) It is necessary to distinguish such things as the terms on which (say) the household (or firm) thinks it can trade from the terms on which it can actually trade, (b) It is necessary to distinguish the terms on which it thinks it can borrow from those on which it actually can borrow, (c) The household (or firm) will have commitments and obligations to others who in turn will have commitments or obligations to it, (d) Some attention must be paid to the consequences of a failure to meet its obligations, i.e. it may become bankrupt. To say that a household's (or firm's) expenditure must be financed out of income, the running down of cash balances, the sale of assets, the incurring of new debts, or by going bankrupt, is to propound a triviality. It is true by definition and is not, therefore, a con-

straint. But somehow to say less than this is to enunciate something which is not true. The household (or firm) faces constraints which it may feel obliged to try to meet, but these are not quite mandatory, in that it is possible to discuss meeting them or not. Constraints in pure theory are treated as mathematically compelling, but these constraints in practice are not. Yet we would surely all agree that households (and firms) are both constrained and act as if they are constrained. It is all rather a puzzle.

[3] D. Ott and A. Ott, 'Budget balance and equilibrium income', *Journal of Finance,* March 1965. Carl Christ, 'A short run aggregate-demand model of the interdependence and effects of monetary and fiscal policies with Keynesian and classical interest elasticities', *American Economic Review,* May 1967. Alan Blinder and Robert Solow, 'Analytical foundations of fiscal policy', in A. Blinder *et al., The Economics of Public Finance,* Brookings Institute, 1974. An excellent survey of the literature is provided by D. Currie, 'Macroeconomic policy and government financing: a survey of recent developments', in M. J. Artis and A. Nobay (eds.), *Studies in Contemporary Economic Analysis,* Croom Helm, 1978.

[4] I hasten to add that I include myself in these strictures.

[5] *Vide* D. Moggridge, *op. cit.,* vol. XIV, pp. 86–100, and D. H. Robertson, *op. cit.,* especially chapters X, XI, XIII and XV.

[6] Blinder and Solow, *op. cit.,* pp. 45 *et seq.*

[7] D. Coppock, 'Some thoughts on the monetary approach to the balance of payments', *Manchester School,* September 1978. D. Currie, 'Some criticisms of the monetary analysis of balance of payments correction', *Economic Journal,* September 1976. W. Branson, 'The dual roles of the government budget and the balance of payments in the movement from short-run to long-run equilibrium', *Quarterly Journal of Economics,* August, 1976.

[8] F. Cripps and W. Godley, 'A formal analysis of the Cambridge Economic Policy Group model', *Economica,* November 1976. See also R. Smith, 'Demand management and the New School', *Applied Economics,* 1976.

[9] This is perfectly apparent in Keynes's own writing.

[10] *Vide* Keynes, *The General Theory of Employment, Interest and Money* (Macmillan, 1936), especially chapters 20 and 21. Note that, while Keynes regards full employment as a

maximum, he adds, 'For a time at least, rising prices may delude entrepreneurs into increasing employment beyond the level which maximises their individual profit measured in terms of the product' (p. 290).

[11] M. Friedman, 'The role of monetary policy', *American Economic Review*, May 1968; reprinted in *The Optimum Quantity of Money* (Macmillan, 1969), chapter 5.

[12] M. Friedman, *op. cit.*, p. 104.

[13] An example of the problem of providing a satisfactory interpretation of the natural rate is contained in the admirable survey by A. M. Santomero and J. J. Seater, 'The inflation—unemployment trade-off: a critique of the literature' (*Journal of Economic Literature*, June 1978). They are most explicit in telling us (p. 515), 'The equilibrium rate of unemployment, commonly called the natural rate, is determined by real phenomena such as market frictions, real income, tax rates, and unemployment compensation. Assuming market equilibria to be unique – a common albeit unverified assumption – any vector of real forces determines a unique equilibrium or natural rate of unemployment. Should the vector of real forces change, the natural rate is likely to change too. Thus, the natural rate clearly is not fixed or constant.' I cannot resist pointing out that, if uniqueness is assumed, it is bound to follow. More seriously, once the vector of real forces is as wide as this, it cannot be assumed that the equilibrium is a function of the real wage, certainly not of the real wage as actually measured. The problem arises in a practical way in D. Laidler's valiant attempt to account for the U.K. inflation of the past decade and a half. He needs so many auxiliary hypotheses in his attempt to bring the natural rate hypothesis to bear that he is in danger of ending up with no degrees of freedom, so to speak. Let me add that I am not denying that the full employment level of unemployment may have risen a little in the late 1960s or early 1970s, merely pointing out how dangerous it is to move into this area of discourse. (D. Laidler, 'Inflation in Britain: a monetarist perspective', *American Economic Review*, September 1976; G. Fane, 'Inflation in Britain: a monetarist perspective: comment', and D. Laidler, Inflation in Britain: a monetarist perspective: reply', both in *American Economic Review*, September 1978.)

[14] It is important to formulate this proposition extremely carefully. Once the economy is in a deficient demand equili-

brium (or disequilibrium), expansion of employment and a fall in unemployment can, and tend to, go hand in hand with a constant or rising real wage. An obvious reason for this is that firms are off their demand curves for labour, i.e. they do not adjust real wages upwards to correspond to lower levels of employment. In practice this means that markets are far from being perfectly competitive.

[15] This was well understood by economists and others involved in the formulation of full employment policy. W. Beveridge (*Full Employment in a Free Society,* Allen & Unwin, 1944) does say, 'The labour market should always be a seller's market rather than a buyer's market' (pp. 18–19).

[16] Although many economists have argued that the possibility should be taken seriously: D. Robertson, *Lectures on Economic Principles* (Fontana, 1963), Part III, chapter II. See also F. Hayek, *Prices and Production* (Routledge, 1931), p. 89: 'It would appear rather that the fall in prices proportionate to the increase in productivity, which necessarily follows when, the amount of money remaining the same, production increases, is not only entirely harmless, but is in fact the only means of avoiding misdirections of production.'

[17] 'Professor Dennis Robertson . . . has warned me that the form of the book may suggest that I am in favour of attacking the problem of unemployment by manipulating wages rather than by manipulating demand. I wish, therefore, to say clearly that this is not so.' (A. C. Pigou, *Lapses from Full Employment,* Macmillan, 1944, p. v.)

[18] Keynes's remark that in the long run we are all dead is usually treated as a joke. It is actually a fundamental proposition of macro-economics, and makes clear *a,* if not *the,* vital difference between Keynesian and classical economics.

[19] Many economists have argued that the Phillips curve has a vertical sector at full employment and a horizontal sector at substantial unemployment with a negatively sloped sector in between, e.g. O. Eckstein and R. Brimmer, *The Inflation Process in the United States* (Joint Economic Committee, 1972). I refer here and in the text to the Phillips curve set out in the article by A. W. Phillips, 'The relation between unemployment and the rate of change of money wage rates in the U.K., 1861–1957' (*Economica,* 1958). I must, however, remind the reader of the earlier discussion of this subject by A. J. Brown, *The Great Inflation 1939–1951* (Cambridge

University Press, 1955). He provides the appropriate data both for the U.K. and U.S., coupling the data with an analysis that shows full awareness of most of the relevant theoretical considerations.

[20] Essentially, if firms mistakenly assume they can raise prices and lower real wages, or labour mistakenly assume that prices will not rise as much as money wages, there will be a temporary rise in employment. A rather obvious criticism of this kind of theorising is that it is based on rather arbitrary assumptions concerning the temporal sequence of input and output prices. The direction of supply responses depends on which changes first, but either could, and, perhaps, *on average* neither does.

[21] W. Beveridge was well aware of the problem of inflation at full employment and the need for a prices and incomes policy not too far distant from a social contract to help control it. He well appreciated the difficulties, but in the light of recent experience was too optimistic about our ability to overcome them. *Op. cit.,* pp. 198–203.

[22] It is extremely surprising that economists have tended to ignore game theoretic ideas when studying problems of macroeconomics. A notable exception is M. Shubik, 'A business cycle model with organised labour considered' (*Econometrica,* April, 1952). For an elementary account of game theory see M. Peston and A. Coddington, *The Elementary Ideas of Game Theory* (Centre for Administrative Studies Occasional Paper No. 6, 1967).

[23] The best account of this is to be found in T. W. Hutchinson, *A Review of Economic Doctrines* (Clarendon, 1953) pp. 324–8.

Chapter Three

Chapter I referred to changes in the underlying structure of the economy, and to whether they might influence the way the system as a whole worked. Foremost among such changes is the influence of economics itself. An economy in which employers and employees (or their representatives) are bombarded with economic data, forecasts and analysis is different from one in which these matters are known only to a tiny minority. Many individuals have an understanding (or think they do) of the way the economic system works. More to the point, organisations either of employers or employees can demand economic expertise and advice if they need it.

Of course, not all forecasts or pieces of applied analysis are published. Especially at the most micro level, commercial secrecy is still maintained. But at the macro level the position is much more open, both with respect to possibilities and with respect to likelihoods. At the very least, people have more knowledge and a better understanding of what is happening in the economy, and, while they will obviously continue to be surprised by new developments, their expectations are not entirely random or ignorant.

Concerning government forecasts, these are not published in all countries, and, even in those that do publish something, it is not necessarily the forecasts that decision-makers really believe in that are given the light of day. None the less, for a variety of reasons the forecasting methods of Economic

Ministries are not kept secret. To start with, all forecasters have the same academic training and background. It is very doubtful whether any fundamental advances in this field have come from government econometricians or statisticians. If they did, it would be hard for them to keep the discovery to themselves for very long, even if they wished to. Apart from anything else, almost all discoveries are multiples, which virtually guarantees their appearing in the public domain before much time elapses. Beyond this, economists in the public sector need to maintain contact with their fellows elsewhere in order to keep themselves up to date with the latest developments. Indeed, for this purpose they will frequently employ outside advisers and consultants. Finally, there is mobility from the public sector to the private, which guarantees that the methods of the public sector can hardly be kept permanently secret.

What all this amounts to is that not only does the Treasury model become available to outsiders, but so do Treasury methods of using it. Even if the Treasury forecast is kept secret, therefore, it is possible to duplicate it with a fair margin of accuracy.[1]

A similar point holds about policy itself. Although the macro-economic policy to be pursued at any time cannot be predicted exactly, the broad policy options available can be assessed by the informed outsider. Even if the best policy experts are in the Treasury (a debatable point at any time), the difference between them and academic and journalist 'amateurs' is only one of degree.

All this can best be put negatively. It would be extra-ordinary if policy-makers' and outsiders' views on the following matters showed consistently wide differences:

1 The likely future short-term development of the key macro-economic variables.
2 The available policy instruments and their efficacy.
3 The objectives to be considered.

I do not mean by this that all policy-makers and all outsiders agree, and I recognise that changes in policy measures
and objectives will emanate from inside government and will
often surprise outsiders. What is apparent is that the Treasury
position will (indeed, must) be inside the range of informed
opinion and not outside it.

Even if the Treasury were to regard its role as one of playing
a zero sum game against all others in the economy, the fact
that it would adopt a mixed strategy is not the same as saying
that its actions are completely unpredictable. Quite the contrary; it would imply that it would be possible to estimate the
probability distribution that determined its choice of strategy.
But, beyond that, it is hard to rationalise the role of the
Treasury as being solely in conflict with the rest of the
economy. The economic process is a partially co-operative
variable sum game.[2] In this case the Treasury will be extremely
keen that many, but not all, of its actions are predictable up
to some degree of accuracy.

What this amounts to is that the economy in the past four
decades has moved from a system in which people largely
reacted to events, and especially those that impinged on them
directly, to a system in which some people endeavour to
analyse and predict events in the large. This shift may have the
ultimate purpose of interpreting their or their organisation's
immediate experience with a view to making money or im-
proving their position in some other way. But the vital thing
about it is that it happens, and is most likely to influence the
way the economy works.

Consider, for example, the behaviour of a trade union. Even
if it is assumed that the wage variable it is interested in is the
real wage, its practical behaviour must be largely to concentrate
on the money wage. The method by which it focuses on a real
wage is to adjust to price changes, probably with a lag. In these
circumstances the appropriate model might be of the form that
desired money wages are adjusted upwards to meet desired

real wages and to compensate for past price changes. As the union becomes more sophisticated the lags on prices will change so that its behaviour will be more and more influenced by recent experience. Assume the average rate of inflation rises by a given percentage. There will be effective money illusion until workers take full cognisance of this and adjust their demands to it. The more rapidly they adjust, the shorter the period of effective money illusion.

It is easy to see, therefore, that, if the way the economy works depends on these intervals of money illusion, its behaviour will actually change as trade unions' perceptions and reactions to the acceleration of the price index change. But the point can be taken further. Trade unions may switch from looking backwards to looking forwards. Having adjusted fully to past events, they may then base their wage demands on forecasts of prices. Thus a rise of this month's price level by a given percentage may be taken to augur a move to a wholly new level of inflation. It is, therefore, not at all inconceivable that money wage demands enter a phase where they rise by more than recent price increases. Instead of an interval of effective money illusion, there may be an interval of what might be termed real income illusion (i.e. people behave as if their real income is lower than it is, rather than higher). Thus, the way the economy works may change yet again.

There is no intellectual difficulty in now going on to the next stage, in which the union and its advisers consider what determines prices. They may predict that existing trends and policies will lead to a devaluation of sterling, which in turn will raise prices. They may then put in for wage increases ahead of the price increases, implying a further behavioural variation for the economic system.

Thus, we have four phases:

1   Trade unions react to events slowly and weakly.
2   Trade unions react to events rapidly and strongly.

3   Trade unions react to forecasts of a naive kind.
4   Trade unions react to forecasts of a sophisticated kind
     based on economic theory and using econometric
     methods.[3]

The general point is that this will be true of all groups in
society and, therefore, the very way the economy behaves and
policy works will change drastically over time. Hence, it is
perfectly reasonable to argue, for example, that devaluation
was an appropriate policy for dealing with a balance of payments deficit in the 1960s, but ceased to be so in the 1970s.

The fact that there is a learning process in the economy,
and part of that learning process centres around the formation
of expectations, is characterised nowadays under the heading
of 'rational expectations theory'.[4] It seems to be made up of
two parts: (a) people revise their expectations in the light of
experience, and (b) people are reflective about the way they
do this so that they do not willingly persist in the same errors.
It is the latter which is vitally important, but, before pursuing
the point, it is important to emphasise that the proposition that
the way the economy is thought to work influences how it
does work is not a new one. What is new is the emphasis
placed on it.

Thus it is a commonplace of Keynesian fiscal policy that
private expenditure functions (and especially the marginal
efficiency of capital) would reflect the cyclical behaviour of
the economy and the average degree of capacity utilisation.
It follows that, if firms believe that the government can avoid
recessions and will do so, their propensity to invest will be
higher on average. This in itself lowers the required degree of
actual fiscal intervention, in principle even to zero. Note
that both parts of the hypothesis are required; belief in the
government's willingness to act and confidence in its ability
to do so. The reverse possibility then also holds, namely that
a recession can result from lack of faith in the government's
capacity to deal with one or in its intention to do so.[5]

All that is old stuff. What needs to be discussed is how important it really is, and whether (as we have already indicated) it has a tendency to become more significant over time.

Consider, for example, an economic variable which is determined by its own past value and a random shock consisting of a first-order auto-regressive process. The optimum forecast for this variable, given a knowledge of the whole stochastic process, is such that the difference between the forecast and the out-turn shows no serial correlation. If, however, the people whose behaviour this process is supposed to represent form their expectations by an adaptive procedure (e.g. change their expenditure by a fraction of the difference between the last expectation and out-turn), there will be a systematic error of forecast. Typically, individuals will underestimate change in either direction and allow the past to influence their expectations for too long. The fundamental question is, will they not notice this, and change their behaviour accordingly? Even if they are unable to estimate the model that generates the variable under consideration, or determine within it an optimum forecast, will they not behave as if they do? In particular, in so far as it is profitable to forecast, will not some individuals forecast successfully so as to make a profit, and will not the competitive process act so as to eradicate the profitability of such forecasts at the margin? In general terms, if a model or theory makes assumptions about expectations and the way they are formed, and that model or theory itself generates forecasts about the variables under consideration, should not the forecasts and expectations be compatible?

The logic of all this is easily set out:

1   We construct a theory of the way people behave.
2   Given that theory, we predict that the economic system will operate in a certain way.
3   The out-turn of the economic system contradicts the assumptions on which individual behaviour was based.

4   People can recognise the divergence between their fore-
     casts and the outcomes.
5   They are capable of analysing these differences, or of pay-
     ing for and understanding expert analysis of true dif-
     ferences.
6   Decision-makers will adjust their behaviour accordingly.

To summarise, there should be a consistency between the
way the economy is thought to work, predictions of its future
development, and the assumptions and forecasts on which
individual actions are based. It must be added immediately
that this does not mean identity of opinion on these matters
at any moment, but it does imply that, to the extent that
forecasts and economic analysis matter, those which are systematically superior have survival value and will come to
dominate those which are systematically inferior.

A further point to add is that we are referring in all cases
to what can be forecast or what can be analysed. In our earlier
example we posited a variable determined by a stationary
stochastic process. In that case there is no mystery about its
path through time, the limits to forecasting being given by
the random new event at time t. A second limit will be lack
of knowledge of the stochastic process, since the time series
from which it can be inferred may be very short. In this case
for quite a while there will be a divergence of view concerning
what is the optimal or rational forecast. But it must be agreed
that, if the process remains the same for long enough, either
explicitly or implicitly the optimum forecast will become
common property and will dominate relevant behaviour.

Central to further discussion, therefore, is whether the
economic system is correctly to be represented by a stationary
stochastic process, which is itself unchanging for long enough
to be discoverable.[6] But, whether or not that is the case, it
still remains true that superior forecasting ability should
dominate inferior, that reflective decision-makers would try
to offset systematic error, and that forecasts which lead to

profit-making opportunities would be offset by the taking of those opportunities, wherever possible.

As a practical example consider the behaviour of a roulette wheel. In a not very efficient casino the wheel may become unbalanced although the proprietors do not notice it. Suppose an individual does notice it, so that he is able to forecast the out-turn better than anybody else. As a result he will be able to make a systematic profit from the wheel, which can be unbounded if the rules of the casino so allow. If he is not short of funds himself, he may have enough to win and to accumulate a larger sum. Alternatively he can sell his information to a wealthier gambler. But all this can only be temporary: (a) other gamblers may discover the imbalance in the wheel, (b) other gamblers will notice the consistent winning of the original discoverer, (c) the casino management will notice its consistent losses. In sum, the new information becomes common property, and behaviour adjusts appropriately.

The essential points are threefold: (a) the ability to forecast in the first place, (b) the eventual public nature of the forecast, (c) the erosion of the return to forecasting by profit-seeking activity. My own view is that these considerations are of great significance for macro-economics in both positive and negative directions. In particular, they bring the two central questions into extremely sharp focus. Firstly, given this view of forecasting, why does the economic system fluctuate and spend so much time away from full employment non-inflationary equilibrium? Secondly, what is it about macro-economic policy that causes it to be effective?

Before commenting on these questions there is another matter that must be raised. The literature of the subject places most of its emphasis on statistics and econometrics. What about economics? Just as there may have to be a consistency between the expectations and the forecasts of a model based on them, does there not have to be a consistency between behaviour and the structure of a model based on it?

If everybody reacts to events as if he believes that the quantity theory of money were true, does not a model of the economy have to include or at least be compatible with the quantity theory of money?[7] If reflective individual decision-makers believe that certain kinds of external shock lead to output contraction in the economy at large, does not a satisfactory model of the economy have to be based on a theory giving rise to such a prediction?

What these considerations mean is that a *theory* about the way the economy works must also be compatible with the determination of expectations and the resulting behaviour of individual people. Firms and households decide what to do by interpreting their experience. These interpretations give rise to actual behaviour, which in turn determines that experience. Now for some individuals, those who concentrate on their own immediate experience, all that is necessary is for events, as they see them directly, not to be in conflict with their interpretations. But for other individuals what is necessary is for the events in the economy as a whole not to be in obvious conflict with what they believe correct macro-economic theory to be.

We are led therefore, to very deep issues of the relationship between beliefs, expectations, decisions, and the outcome of those decisions. In particular, since not all theoretical beliefs are the same, the question must be asked whether and in what circumstances certain theoretical beliefs have survival value. Such questions lie at the very heart of the difference between natural and social science. Social scientific theories are part of their own domain of discourse.[8] In our context economic theories are themselves one of the givens of the economy, and methods of investigating, testing and disseminating them are part of its structure. If people believe that the quantity theory of money is true, do they behave in a way which makes it true? If people believe that the economy is a self-equilibrating system, does that help the economy to move towards equilibrium? If it does not, will they change their minds, and believe that the economy is not a self-equilibrating system? In the latter case will this ensure that the economy shows no tendency to offset deviations from full employment? Beyond that, how do the answers to these questions depend on the number of people who hold certain economic principles? Do they depend on the economic power of those people?

In sum, it has been argued that the expectations on which our econometric model has been based should not differ from the forecasts produced by that model. For completeness it must be argued that the theoretical basis for the formation of those expectations must be logically equivalent to the theoretical foundations on which that econometric model is built.

Let us, therefore, consider the following classification of theories:

1   Potentially survivable theories are ones which hold when it is known that they are believed to hold.
2   Potentially non-survivable theories are ones which do not hold when it is publicly known that they are believed to hold.
3   Theories the truth of which does not depend on whether or not they are believed to hold.

We may clarify the concept of survival to mean survival for a given number of years, or survival relative to at least *n* people believing them to hold. We may also divide 'theory' into two categories: general theory of an abstract nature, and specific testable and tested hypotheses.

Can we cite examples of these theory types? One has already been mentioned. Suppose it is believed that devaluation works by raising the price of U.K.-produced goods and foreign goods relative to U.K. money wages. The foreign balance improves and reserves of foreign exchange are built up while this real wage effect occurs, subject to the condition that

domestic capacity is switched to the production and away
from the consumption of tradables. If it happens that trade
unions believe the theory and adjust their money wage
behaviour so that they predict the price effects of the
devaluation, at best it may not work at all, and, at worst, will
cause a deterioration in the balance of payments. Of course,
at a higher level it could be argued that the theory stands up.
Only the parameters within which it operates have changed.
But that is to miss the point that those parameters are actually
dependent on the theory, and it no longer remains a proposition of economics that devaluation influences the balance
of payments in the way it was supposed to.

If we consider monetary theory especially in its international context, another sort of conclusion can be reached.
Let it be argued that domestic credit expansion must lead
to a rise in the price level and a decline in the rate of exchange.
The theoretical basis of this may be to do with expenditure
out of higher money balances leading to nominal (and possibly
real) income expansion, and a deterioration of the balance of
payments. If firms know and believe the theory, however, they
may act as if its predictions were bound to happen and mark
up prices and sell sterling short in ways that accelerate its
outcome. Thus domestic credit expansion, even in conditions
of under-capacity working, may have few real effects and
powerful money effects just because of people's beliefs.

The validity of this theory in its strong form depends on
belief in it. It is easy to see that after a while the theory may
be subject to critical scrutiny, and it may be argued successfully that its inflationary effects 'really' depend on a most
complicated process of real effects. If people become convinced of that, the theory may revert to its weak form, so that
DCE will have real effects at less than full employment and
inflationary effects only later as the trade balance deteriorates
and full employment is reached.

There is no need to stop at this point. If firms and trade

union leaders are sophisticated enough to understand economic analysis and interpret the results of econometric models, they are also capable of understanding the connection between their beliefs and the way the economy works. In our previous example, speculators and others can see that whether DCE is rapidly inflationary or not depends on whether decision-makers (i.e. themselves) believe it to be. We are now back at Keynes's interpretation of the stock market, successful operations in which he saw as depending on a view of what the market's view was likely to be.[9] The conclusion then becomes the pretty obvious one that the effects of external shocks and the efficacy of policies depend on firms' and households' interpretations of their circumstances in the small and in the large. In particular, this means that they will not always react in precisely the same way.

The next stage of the discussion is to try and put these reflections into some kind of perspective. The major purpose of this is to reconsider the question of the automatic response of the economy to an external shock and the role of public policy.

Let us accept for the sake of argument that the economy has an equilibrium relative to all the external forces operating on it. In broad terms this equilibrium would imply that all plans are realised and all expectations fulfilled. In addition, it would change as these external forces changed. How do we interpret the notion of the economy spending considerable periods of time out of equilibrium?

One way of answering this question is trivial, but some economists come perilously close to giving it. So many external forces are specified, and so many additional conditions laid down, that it almost appears as if the economy is always in equilibrium; or, if not in equilibrium, at least adjusting in an optimal way. This approach merely leads to the substitution of a second, virtually equivalent, question, namely how do we interpret the economy changing its equilibrium with the frequency it does, and are there any invariants within those changes?[10]

I myself prefer the question as usually put, although I recognise that the particular equilibrium state can change. Sticking to that view, the answer in the broadest terms is as follows:

1   The economy is a decentralised system in which the individual unit, be it household, firm, financial institution or bank, can act only for itself or in concert with a number of other units, which are all small relative to the economy as a whole.

2   The forces impinging on the economy are not always readily identifiable or observable.

3   The co-ordinating mechanism of the economy, namely prices set in markets, operates slowly and imperfectly because of the first two assumptions. In particular, the direct effect of an external shock does not appear simultaneously in all markets, and the sequential process of adjustment is further complicated by the interdependence of markets.

4   Market interdependence is of several forms. In so far as decisions depend on relative prices, more than one market is immediately involved even if the issue is the quantity of a single good or service to buy. Many demands are derived demands in that they exist because of a desire to sell in some other market. Beyond that, demand may be supply-constrained, in that what is bought in one market may depend on a transaction in another having already been completed.

5   The economy is a money one, so that, even if goods and services are sold with a view to using the proceeds to buy other goods and services, the proceeds themselves accrue as money which may not be spent immediately. Beyond that, the decision eventually to buy is not signalled im-

mediately to possible suppliers. A particular problem for the price mechanism is to relate decisions in the present to decisions in the future. There may not exist markets in which such information is presented in fine enough detail or can be adjusted to.

I have used the word 'information' here advisedly. It has been argued that the correct way to analyse the economy is as an information-processing system.[11] Markets use information, but extremely economically, to seek out the equilibrium. Disequilibrium exists while this is happening, and may persist because of the limitations of the market mechanism.

It is further argued (and this takes us back to rational expectations) that the market, inefficient though it is, makes the best possible use of information. The mechanism may be imperfect, but that is only so if it is compared to an unattainable ideal. Relative to the way the economy actually works, nothing better is available. (Of course, a different kind of economic system may be superior, although that is doubted by those who propound these pro-market views. But to pursue such a line is to change the rules of the game, which is to consider the dynamics of the existing kind of mixed economy.)

Now, there is a sense in which the problem really seems to be one of information. What did the Keynesians mean by effective demand but demand as it reveals itself in the market, as opposed to potential demand as it exists in somebody's mind? In so far as this period's saving really is for future spending the problem is in part to convey the information to firms for whom it matters. Keynesian unemployment may be partially attributable to workers being willing to work at a lower real wage than currently rules but being unable to signal this to employers. They are also trying to signal to employers that if they were taken on they would spend the resulting income and make the production they would undertake a profitable business. It is easy to write parts of Keynesian theory in these terms, but it is doubtful whether anything is contributed thereby other than the semantic change.

All this goes back to Adam Smith and the hidden hand. According to Smith, each decision-maker took a narrow view of his objectives and acted accordingly. The individual might have been seeking his own equilibrium and his own welfare. Nobody sought general equilibrium or national welfare, but the system behaved as if they did. Unfortunately, although Smith's concept was of fundamental importance, and the possibility of the hidden hand was a major breakthrough in thought, he himself was unable to show rigorously that the hand worked as well as he claimed. Moreover the job has still not been carried out satisfactorily in theory, let alone established in practice.[12]

The system may not minimise welfare or fly wildly away from equilibrium. As a mechanism it is not *too* bad, but the presumption that it moves towards full employment is far from established. The facts indicate that it is rather sluggish and hardly the clockwork so beloved of eighteenth-century thinkers. Moreover the reason for this is not obviously lack of information.

Let us bear in mind that the decentralised system is supposed to be extremely economical in its use of information. But add to that modern economic knowledge. Suppose an all-knowing observer could analyse a random shock and predict the equilibrium outcome. Would his announcement of the outcome move the economy to that equilibrium?

While not denying that the announcement might have an effect both on expectations and behaviour, it is not apparent that the equilibrium would necessarily be reached. The reason is that, even if the equilibrium were known, individuals still do not have the power to act to reach it. Indeed, the more decentralised the system the less power any individual has to pursue on his own any policy which might help in the move to equilibrium.

To put the point in contemporary terms, deficient information on the equilibrium of the U.K. economy is not what lies behind the system's failure to move away from its present circumstances, in which for all practical purposes it is stuck. Certainly the economy is behaving as if it is lost and does not know where to go, but it is the behaviour which is significant. The rest is analogy.

I myself would now want to take the argument further than that. I agree that, in so far as the lack of certainty in the economy is characterised by a stationary stochastic process, the private sector is just as capable of discovering this as anybody else. Also, in so far as forecasting is about the prediction of such a stochastic process, the private sector is capable of forecasting optimally. Beyond that, if such forecasting opens up opportunities for profitable speculation the result will be to take them and, thereby, eradicate them, leaving the typical forecast errors as unpredictably random, and not systematic *ex ante.*

I would then add two further considerations. One is that not all lack of certainty is risk (in Knight's sense). Much of it *is* uncertainty. Secondly, in any case strategies may not be available to the private sector to make use of forecasts and respond correctly to uncertain shocks.

The problem of behaviour is actually quite central to the working of the hidden hand. A classic question in competition theory used to be 'If all the firms in a competitive industry have perfect knowledge, why do they not know that monopolistic behaviour is more profitable to them?'. The answer is that they do know it, but they cannot make use of their knowledge. We have the usual paradox that, if each knows that all the rest will keep their output restrained, his best policy is to cut his price and sell more. But they all know this, which means they do not trust each other. But they all know that too, so that they ought to be able to rely on each other. The regress is infinite, and is actually not limited just to pure competition. The prisoner's dilemma game shows that it applies to small groups too.[13] Knowledge implies neither optimality, nor stability, nor even the existence of an equilibrium.

Consider the economy in a Keynesian under-employment equilibrium. Firms may be aware that there is under-employment, the reason being deficient demand: demand for labour and that for final output being interdependent. Let us go further and agree that they may even know how existing real wages compare with full-employment real wages. In other words, each individual decision-maker is apprised of those macro-economic facts which at best could be available to the omniscient external observer. Does this cause the system to move to equilibrium? The answer is surely in the negative, because the equilibrium still depends on all firms pursuing a correct policy for themselves, which no individual firm can rely on. The individual firm's position is exactly what it was before, namely being unable to sell capacity output, unwilling to hire as many employees as it used to, and not certain whether to cut price. Similarly, the individual worker is unable to find a job as easily as before, and may be out of a job altogether. He too does not know whether and to what extent to moderate his money wage demands.

It is precisely at this point that the role of the government appears. It is exactly the role that Keynes and the Keynesians have always argued for, to do for the economy what it cannot do for itself.

This may be in two forms: (a) where possible to improve the automatic mechanism or hidden hand, (b) where necessary to replace the hidden hand with direct intervention.

I hasten to add that this is the stabilising role of the government. In addition, there is the size of the public sector at full employment, which is much more a matter of social and political policy (or political economy) than of technical macro-economic policy. The two may be related, however. If it is believed, as it was by many people in the 1930s, that the capitalist system has a chronic tendency towards stagnation, public expenditure may be a necessary component of full employment independent of its other desirable characteristics. Beyond that, as we have remarked earlier, mistakes of public policy at full employment (notably a tendency to exaggerate the desire of workers to trade off private consumption for public consumption or investment) can be destabilising.

I have stated that the approach via information provides few substantive insights and is really rather semantic. The orthodox view of macro-economic policy remains, therefore, the correct one in the abstract. Nonetheless, the new analysis of expectations leads to a serious reconsideration of the efficacy of policy.

To take this problem further let us revert to the simple models of Chapter I. Rewrite them to take account of expectations as follows:

$$x_t = a\hat{x}_t + by_{t-1} + z_t \qquad\qquad 1$$

where $\hat{\ }$ refers to the value of x_t as expected in period $t-1$, and y is a policy instrument.

x_t may be real income and $a\hat{x}_t$ real private expenditure. Alternatively, x_t may be the rate of change of the price level and $\hat{x}_t$ the expected rate of change. Obviously, this simple model avoids a great many difficulties, and behind it will be a most complex reality. But we can still use it to make our main points.

The first question to ask is, how will this system behave if the policy variable is kept constant? Essentially, x_t will fluctuate as a, $\hat{x}_t$ and z_t fluctuate. For example, if $\hat{x}_t$ is related to past values of x_t, the system will show dynamics partly because of the behaviour of z_t, and partly because of the connection between x_t and its earlier values. In appropriate circumstances the system will vary in a stable fashion about the mean value of $z_t + by$.

Suppose now that z_t follows a serially uncorrelated stationary stochastic process. Let us redefine x_t as the deviation of the dependent variable from $by + E(z_t)$. We may rewrite equation 1 as follows:

$$x_t = a\,\hat{x}_t + z_t \qquad\qquad 2$$

where $E(z_t) = 0$ by assumption. It now follows that

$$E(x_t) = a\,E(\hat{x}_t) \qquad\qquad 3$$

A proposition of rational expectations theory is that $E\,\hat{x}_t = x_t = \hat{x}_t$. In this case, it would follow that $\hat{x}_t = 0$. The system would then behave as

$$x_t = z_t \qquad\qquad 4$$

It would fluctuate around its mean as a serially uncorrelated random process. Public policy would have influenced its average level, but not its dynamic stability. It would actually be as stable as possible, which implies that continually varying the policy instrument can only make the system less stable.

Consider now the possibility that z_t is a stationary stochastic process, but an autocorrelated one. It is now vital to distinguish its unconditional expectation from its conditional one. It behaves according to the following process.

$$z_t = e_t + c\,e_{t-1} \qquad\qquad 5$$

where e_t is a serially uncorrelated stationary stochastic process with zero mean. The unconditional expectation of z_t is equal to $(1 + c)Ee_t$, which we take to be $(1 + c)e$, i.e. zero. The conditional expectation of z_t after the random shock has occurred at time e_{t-1} is $e + c\,e_{t-1}$ where e_{t-1} has occurred.

Let us again redefine x_t and deduct by plus the unconditional expectation of z_t from x_t as initially defined. Let us also redefine y_t as the deviation from its mean. The system may then be written as follows

$$x_t = a\hat{x}_t + e_t + c\,e_{t-1} \qquad 6$$

Consider the conditional expectation of x_t at time $t-1$.

$$E(x_t/t-1) = a\,E(\hat{x}_t/t-1) + E(e_t) + c\,E(e_{t-1}/t-1) + by_{t-1} \qquad 7$$

$$= a\,E(\hat{x}_t/t-1) + c\,e_{t-1} + by_{t-1}$$

(where $E(x_t/t-1)$ means the conditional expectation of a variable at time $t-1$). In this case the condition $E(x_t/t-1) = E(\hat{x}_t/t-1)$ implies

$$E(\hat{x}_t/t-1) = \hat{x}_t = \frac{c}{1-a}e_{t-1} + \frac{b}{1-a}y_{t-1} \qquad 8$$

It would then follow that

$$x_t = e_t + \frac{c}{1-a}e_{t-1} + \frac{b}{1-a}y_{t-1} = e_t + \hat{x}_t \qquad 9$$

In this case x_t would fluctuate, but there would be no serial correlation in the errors of forecast, $x_t - \hat{x}_t$. The difference now is that it appears that y can be used as a stabilising instrument. Suppose by_{t-1} varies around its mean level according to the formula $-ce_{t-1}$. We would then have x_t equal to zero, with the result that

$$x_t = a\hat{x}_t + e_t \qquad 10$$

In other words, we would be back with our first case, but the reason would now be the stabilising policy of the government. The economy would then appear to be at optimum stability, partly because of optimum stabilisation policy and partly because of the optimum forecasts of income on which private expenditure is based. The optimum assessment of the policy instrument is precisely what private expectations take into account. Note that in these circumstances the government, although engaged in active policymaking, is following a rule. Since the rule involves a reaction to circumstances, there is the interesting question whether or not this is correctly to be described as discretionary policy. It should also be appreciated that the behaviour of the government is predictable, which is what allows the private sector to predict optimally but does not render the policy itself nugatory.

The sort of model to which the rational expectations hypothesis is applied is one of price inflation.[14] Let P be the rate of change of prices, Q the rate of change of output, M the rate of the change of the policy instrument (e.g. the quantity of money). Let $\hat{}$ over a variable refer to the expectation of its value, e.g. $\hat{P}$ is the expectation of the rate of change of prices. A typical model of inflation is as follows.

$$P = aM + (1-a)\hat{P} \qquad 11$$

$$Q = b(M - \hat{P}) \qquad 12$$

i.e. the inflation rate increases when the quantity of money rises faster than expected prices, and output also rises more rapidly (perhaps relative to some underlying rate).

From the first equation the expected value of P is given by

$$E(P) = a E(M) + (1-a) E(\hat{P}). \qquad 13$$

If we assume $E(P) = \hat{P} \; (= E\hat{P})$, we conclude

$$\hat{P} = E(M) \qquad 14$$

Inserting this is equation 11,

$$P = aM + (1-a)E(M) \qquad 15$$

Define M as $E(M) + z$, where z is a random shock.

$$P = E(M) + z \qquad 16$$

If we put the expression for $\hat{P}$ in equation 12 we infer

$$Q = b[M - E(M)] = bz \qquad 17$$

Thus, if there are no 'surprises' in public policy, the target variable P responds to the instrument M, but the alternative target variable Q is unaffected.

Consider now the dual model

$$Q = aM + (1-a)\,\hat{Q} \qquad 18$$

$$P = b(M - \hat{Q}) \qquad 19$$

This says that the rate of increase of output grows when the quantity of money rises faster than expected output, and prices also accelerate.

Since the two models are entirely symmetrical, exactly the same results follow except for name change. In other words, in this model, public policy affects output but influences prices only if it is surprising.

What are we to make of this? It is clear that the rational expectations hypothesis depends for its substantive effect on the nature of the model. It does, however, in this case lead to a rather interesting, but wholly reassuring, conclusion.

If we ask why equation 11 should hold, the answer must be that people accept the theory that increases in the quantity of money increase prices and not output. In other words, the conditions for the elementary quantity theory hold and are believed to hold and the quantity theory itself follows. If we ask the same question about equation 18, the answer must be that people accept the theory that increases in the quantity of money increase output and not prices. In other words, the conditions for the elementary Keynesian theory hold and are believed to hold, and the Keynesian theory itself follows. In sum, rational expectations theory tells us what we started off with, that sometimes one simple model is applicable and sometimes the other.

There is one additional point to add. If the influence of a policy instrument is set out in the theory as depending on the difference between that instrument *ex post* and its value *ex ante,* naturally enough when the two are the same the instrument will have no effect. If, moreover, the *ex ante* value is defined as the mathematical expectation of the *ex post* value, then again the rational expectations hypothesis holds that an instrument has an effect only when its actual value differs from its expected value. Further still, if the difference between the expectations and the out-turn is referred to as the unexpected part of the instrument, then the conclusion follows inevitably that only the unexpected part of policy has an effect.

This leads to two remarks. First, surely it is not necessarily the case that the influence of an instrument depends on the difference between its values *ex ante* and *ex post*. It is reasonable to argue that the reverse could just as easily be true, that influence depends on the *ex ante* value being the same as the *ex post* one. Second, the concept of unexpectedness is purely semantic and has no deeply explored significance. It is simply a word for the forecast error. Once more it could fairly be argued that people who are clever enough to predict as well as the rational expectations hypothesis requires must know that out-turns differ from forecasts in a stochastic world. Thus the forecast error is not at all unexpected. What would be unexpected or surprising, to use Shackle's terminology, would be the non-appearance of forecast errors.

Nonetheless, within the broad rational expectations framework we can take a few more steps forward. The first is to appreciate the reliance which is placed on the private sector's ability to use the model of the economy and make a conditional forecast. To the extent to which it is unable to do this it forecasts will show systematic errors. If the underlying statistical regime changes, private sector forecasts may be suboptimal or irrational for a while. This time period could easily be long enough to generate cycles. A related point concerns the operation of the feedback rule. The shock, e_{t-1}, cannot be observed but needs to be estimated. The government may be able to do this more quickly and efficiently than the private sector, and be able to act more effectively on the basis of the information. The question of action remains of overwhelming significance although it is submerged within the aggregate model. Even if the private sector could forecast optimally and knew the government's policy rule, it still might not be able to respond appropriately at the level of market behaviour. It might behave, therefore, as if it did not forecast rationally, even if the rational forecast for the economy at large were published. This would add some additional dynamics to the system's response and leave more room for active policy.

The final point to raise is whether the expectational calculus is, strictly speaking, applicable to this kind of problem. In essence the application of this approach depends on the assumption that lack of certainty is correctly characterised by a stationary stochastic process. If, as I have remarked, we turn instead to the assumption that the lack of certainty is a form of uncertainty not to be expressed in probability terms, the whole notion of converging rationally to a correct prediction becomes suspect. The difficulty with this is that it not only damages rational expectations theory, it also begins to lay waste the whole of the orthodox approach to econometrics.

There are many topics I have not been able to cover in this book. Notable among them is the approach via the analysis of disequilibrium. All I can say on that is that it appears to be very promising, if rather *ad hoc* for the moment.[15] I do, however, wish to say a few words, of a methodological nature, on another recent version of unemployment theory.

The strength of economics derives to a considerable extent from its language, its vocabulary, and its related capacity to formulate problems and theory. Its weaknesses derive from the unobservability of so many of its concepts, and the untestability except in an impossible world of so many of its hypotheses.

Economists, like Humpty Dumpty, use words in their own way. When they say that people are rational they mean either that they do what they want to do, or that what they want to do is revealed by what they actually do. Another version of rationality is that people are consistent in the sense of behaving in a similar fashion in similar circumstances. When they are said to maximise utility or profit, this also turns out to mean that they do what they want to do or are consistent. What is clear is that rationality does not mean the explicit use of reason, the analysis of circumstances, or the attempt to relate cause to effect. Maximisation may involve no mathematical analysis, or no acquaintance with mathematics at all.

Concentrating on the language of economics, although it would be claimed that, just like the subject itself, this is value-free, again, just like the subject itself, it is so only philosophically, not in actual practice. Moreover, although the expert can tell the difference between a semantic change and a substantive one, the outsider cannot. One example of the dangers that arise we have already discussed, namely the natural rate of unemployment. There is nothing 'natural' about the natural rate, if by that is meant inevitable or unchangeable, and there is even less 'natural' about it if by that is meant desirable or the best possible. But the concept, although misleading to the outsider, can be saved within the subject, especially if it is regarded as a not especially original generalisation of what is meant by full employment.

Turning to the search theory of unemployment,[16] the proposition in the new economics that the unemployed man or women is searching for a job does not imply any particular activity on his or her part. When it is said that the unemployed person is sampling job opportunities and acquiring information about the state of and change in the state of the labour market, this implies nothing about his mental condition. Similarly, an employed person is regarded as continuously searching for a superior job, acquiring information all the time. But the most extreme example is the proposition that a worker laid off can be regarded as implicitly rejecting a money wage offer that is implicitly made to him, although no offer is actually made or rejected.

The conclusion is presented that all unemployment is therefore voluntary, but this tells us more about some economists' lack of understanding of the English language than about their ability to make a substantive contribution to the subject. Presumably, firms unable to sell their product are voluntarily not selling it, because implicitly they are rejecting potentially lower bids. More generally, the whole state of the economy outside equilibrium (assuming it exists) is a voluntary one, since implicitly all decision-makers are rejecting whatever they would get in equilibrium. Thus the answer to the question 'Why is there large-scale unemployment, rising inflation and slow growth in the U.K.?' is that the U.K. voluntarily chooses that situation. After all, nobody doubts that superior situations are possible. The argument is reminiscent of so-called proofs that there is no such thing as free choice, or an unselfish act, or a commitment. They present amusing conundrums but no more. Much neo-classical economics consists of theorising without explanation, but it usually has the merit of encompassing the possible facts. Its trouble is its lack of predictive power in that it rules out too few phenomena. Search theory does not even manage that, and for the most part, if taken seriously, and with only a few auxiliary hypotheses, is simply untrue.

My purpose in this book has been to give some kind of perspective for the student of contemporary macro-economics to help us appreciate current developments and older discoveries. I have been conscious of the twin dangers of concentrating on everything that is new and of insisting that there is nothing new under the sun. I am aware also that in concentrating on what interests me personally, and, I hope, on subjects on which I have at least a little to say, I am biased and can be misleading. But I am aware that much more distinguished economists that I can ever aspire to emulate have not been above the most extreme prejudice, and that those who cry loudest about scientific method do not always display the critical spirit.

What, then, is the intellectual position that I actually hold?
It should be apparent that it derives first and foremost from
the works of Keynes. It seems to me that the *General Theory*
remains the dominant work of modern macro-economics, and
that and Keynes's related writings as they have begun to appear
in the *Collected Writings* are overwhelmingly the most
important reading for any serious student. This is not to
underestimate all that has followed. The Keynesian revolution
really did transform economic thinking, and it is not over by a
long way yet.[17]

I readily agree that so impressive was the original achieve-
ment that many economists, the present writer not excluded,
got stuck in their ways. They took too much for granted and
used the income—expenditure approach in a mechanical
fashion. But luckily there are always critics within the profession who open up new problems, or more valuably point
out that old problems have not actually been solved.

Examples of how we have moved forward are those I have
emphasised: the contemporary view of the balance of payments, the importance of the government budget constraint,
and the possibly endogenous nature of expectations. Areas
where we have done less well are the analysis of disequilibrium,
in which there is superb work in progress, and the labour
market, where we seem to know less than when we started.
Above all, conflict and conflict resolution seem vital to the
study of inflation, and stagflation, and yet they are topics
which remain largely untouched by theorists.

I have said nothing about a monetarist counter-revolution.
The reason, as I have already remarked in the Introduction, is
simply that I do not believe there has been one. One part of
what is called monetarism, the tendency of the economy to
reach full employment on its own, is unsubstantiated within
the context of serious discussion.[18] The related point of the
independence of real and monetary phenomena in the long
run was as well established and as irrelevant in the 1930s as

it is today. The possible destabilising role of government, true or false (and as a possibility it is surely true, but as a general rule false), is not dependent specifically on the monetary instrument. Even the contemporary analysis of inflation, now that it has settled down somewhat, gives no greater weight to money than Keynes would have done. This is particularly true if the case that is chiefly examined is the monetary financing of a budget deficit at full employment rather than the nonsense of the thought-experiment of helicopter money. The point holds *a fortiori* if the monetary finance also arises as a means of neutralising the head-on conflict of collective bargaining, converting impossible real demands into sustainable money ones.

On the contention that the labour market is of no special importance it may be remarked that, on the one hand, while this must continue to be subject to empirical test, it seems to go against all experience in the U.K.; on the other hand, in practice hardly anybody who regards himself as a committed monetarist really seems to believe it.[19] Whether the labour market is just like any other market in a sense also depends on the problem in hand — it is for some purposes and is not for others. But it is not apparent how the impact and medium-term effects of trade union wage push can even be examined, let alone tested, if an assumption is not made about the special and far-reaching nature of labour market activities.

My final comments concern economics itself. It is said that events of the past decade have dealt a severe blow to economics as a subject, both because they were not predicted and because no remedies of a relatively painless kind have emerged. 'Predicted' here may mean three things. There may be complaints that economists did not prophesy the development of the Vietnam war or how the U.S. government financed it, or the strengthening of the O.P.E.C. cartel, or the political events in France, or the failure of the Brazilian coffee crop and other harvests. To this they must plead guilty, but add in mitigation that they have never claimed to be able to do so. Quite the contrary: they have always emphasised the significance of the unpredictability of such random shocks. Secondly, it is alleged that economists did not predict the consequences of such shocks. Here there is less need to plead guilty. It took many of us in the profession some time to appreciate their significance (especially their scale), but their main consequences were correctly analysed. There are four exceptions to this, however, which must be stated. Some, chiefly free market, economists predicted that the O.P.E.C. cartel would collapse, and that it was therefore a transitory phenomenon. Some economists did not expect that international economic co-operation, especially by the leading Western powers, would diminish as rapidly and to the extent that has occurred. Few economists thought that inflationary expectations would persist as long as they have. Finally, many economists, if not the majority felt that unemployment levels of recent times would more or less bring trade union wage push to a stop. I am not saying that all economists made all these errors. There may even be some economist somewhere who got everything right. But a reading of the literature, especially of the early 1970s, indicates at least a moderate degree of confusion.

This leads to the third complaint, which is that we lack remedies for our present predicament. Here again, perhaps, a verdict of not proven is the appropriate one. The monetarists certainly claim to have a remedy. It is to control the money supply on an announced and non-inflationary path, and to let the free market (including the international money market) do the rest. Where there are restraints on the free market, these must be abolished, and eventually all will be well. One objection to this is the usual one that the problem is here and now while eventually is too far away. Some other economists see salvation for the U.K., at least, in the control of imports, together with a fiscal stance which is expansionary but which concentrates on the regeneration of manufacturing industry.

Their view is almost the diametric opposite of the monetarists' in that they will actually reduce the role of the free market further and extend that of the bureaucracy. In addition, they do not have a convincing explanation of how they will control inflation when in the short term they are reducing supply and increasing demand.

In between, some of the more orthodox Keynesians see salvation in a moderate degree of fiscal and monetary expansion, an incomes and prices policy, and a return to international economic co-operation. They have accepted that an immediate return to full employment is impossible because of its implications for inflation and the balance of payments, but reject the view that a move in the opposite direction is the best way of making progress. The weakness of their position is twofold: it is extremely difficult to keep prices and incomes policies going long enough to reduce inflation and inflationary expectations so as to allow the other policies to work, and international co-operation tends nowadays to be honoured in the breach. Perhaps the one thing to be said in favour of the mainstream position is that it does devote itself to keeping the patient alive.

Notes

[1] I do not mean by this that the Treasury's forecasts are ground out by the Treasury model. A great many preconditions are stipulated before the model is used, and, as far as I can understand it, the forecasts themselves are doctored (i.e. judgement is applied) at various subsequent stages.

[2] Thus the Treasury sees it as one of its tasks to inform the T.U.C., the C.B.I. and the public at large of what it calls 'the economic facts of life'. Regrettably, it is sometimes limited in what it can do both by political pressures and by the need to influence as far as it can domestic money markets and the international market in sterling.

[3] Just to show that there really does seem to be precious

little that is new in the world, let me cite the following observations made by D. H. Robertson in 1955: 'In Sweden already, according to Professor Lundberg, the trades union movement attempts to forecast the effect of its wage claims on prices and to write up the claim in accordance with a multiplier formula which takes account also of the marginal rate of taxation being higher than the average. Such a multiplier is probably convergent, but may nevertheless be large. And not all such "expectational" processes can be relied upon to converge.' ('Creeping inflation', *Bulletin of the London and Cambridge Economic Service,* 1955.) Unfortunately he himself does not give a reference to substantiate Professor Lundberg's point, but it has been pointed out to me that this is probably *Business Cycles and Economic Policy* (Swedish edition, 1953; Allen & Unwin, 1957).

[4] J. F. Muth, 'Rational expectations and the theory of price movements', *Econometrica,* July 1961. My cynical view is that most economic writing is accepted too soon. This and the first articles on the government budget restraint are the best current examples of works whose impact was delayed excessively.

[5] To pursue the theme of 'the older generation knew it all', let me refer to the following remark of Professor Hayek's: '. . . from a practical point of view, it would be one of the worst things which could befall us if the general public should ever again cease to believe in the elementary propositions of the quantity theory' (*Prices and Production,* Routledge, 1931, p. 3). I must emphasise that in this much neglected work Hayek presents an extremely sophisticated, if controversial, theory of the price level. In addition, to revert to a theme raised by Corry (*supra, op. cit.*), it is hard to see why Hayek did not then go on to produce a macro-theory of output as a whole. Stranger still, Lionel Robbins in his preface to the Hayek volume seemed to understand clearly what was required. He said, 'The forces involved in the equations of equilibrium no longer determine the money receipts of producers. A guarantee that equilibrium will be preserved is no longer given. . . . The monetary theories have been too monetary. They have treated fluctuations in monetary factors as merely general and superficial phenomena. They have totally failed to bring the theory of money into harmony with the theory of production.' (*Ibid.*, pp. viii–ix.) Thus the seeds of modern macro-economics were all there before Keynes. Those who

seek to attack his greatness on that account, however, miss the point. It was precisely Keynes and not the others who was able to make the mental leap and offer the theory of output as a whole in a modern form.

[6] Keynes himself was extremely doubtful of this. A great deal of Part II of his *General Theory of Unemployment* (*Collected Works,* vol. xiv, ed. D. Moggridge) is devoted to emphasising the importance of uncertainty as opposed to risk, which is expressible in probabilistic terms. He refers (p. 114) to matters for which 'there is no scientific basis on which to form any calculable probability whatever. We simply do not know ... How do we manage in such circumstances to behave in a manner which saves our faces as rational, economic men?' Hicks, in 'A suggestion for simplifying the theory of money' (*Economica,* 1935), does use probabilistic notions, as does Myrdal in *Monetary Equilibrium.*

[7] This is the Hayek point referred to above. The philosophical question concerns what causes what, but he did not then and has not subsequently doubted the influence of ideas on society and, therefore, on themselves.

[8] As an example, consider the following comment on the Phillips curve. We may distinguish the following states of the economy:

1   A state in which, although wage changes and unemployment occur, no data on these are collected.
2   A state in which aggregate wage and unemployment statistics are collected and published.
3   A state in which someone relates the two sets of figures and even draws a line between the two.
4   A state in which theories are published about the connection between the two.
5   A state in which the government uses the theories and the fitted curve to influence unemployment levels or money wage changes.
6   A state in which individual firms or households or their representatives take account either of the fitted line or of government policy based on the line in determining their own behaviour.

This is the kind of point that Professor Popper has made much of, yet, rather puzzlingly, he does not see the logic of social scientific discovery as differing from the logic of natural scientific discovery.

[9] In his 1937 article, quoted above, Keynes answers the rationality question partly as follows, 'Knowing that our own individual judgement is worthless, we endeavour to fall back on the judgement of the rest of the world, which is perhaps better informed. That is, we endeavour to conform with the behaviour of the majority on the average. The psychology of a society of individuals each of whom is endeavouring to copy the others leads to what we may strictly term a *conventional* judgement.' (*Op. cit.*, p. 114.)

[10] *Vide* my comment on Laidler *supra*.

[11] Apart from Leijonhufvud, reference may be made to A. Alchian and W. Allen, *University Economics* (third edition, Wadsworth, 1972). An early example of this kind of argument is F. Hayek, 'The use of knowledge in society' (*American Economic Review*, 1945).

[12] I am very struck by F. Hahn's remark, '. . . it will be a consequence of my approach that one can only discuss the stability in the small of an equilbrium . . . What is to be emphasised is that the position which I have adopted makes it impossible to make any global stability claims.' (*On the Notion of Equilibrium in Economics*, Cambridge University Press, 1973, pp. 28–9.)

[13] M. Peston and A. Coddington, *op. cit.*

[14] Examples can be found in D. Laidler, *Essays on Money and Inflation* (Manchester University Press, 1975).

[15] There is an extremely useful collection of articles on this theme in *Scandinavian Journal of Economics*, 1977, No. 2.

[16] The *locus classicus* of this kind of theorising is E. Phelps (ed.), *Micro-economic Foundations of Employment and Inflation Theory* (Norton, 1970).

[17] If I may add a last comment on this theme, surely Keynes's economics was the economics of Keynes. Keynesian elements of a quantity adjustment kind due to such things as 'surprise' within a classical model incorporating expectations are not the same thing. Similarly, theories such as those of Clower or the students of disequilibrium, excellent though they are in themselves, should not automatically be taken as equivalent to or definitive interpretations of the *General Theory*. In this regard I am in agreement with A. Coddington ('Keynesian economics: the search for first principles', *Journal of Economic Literature*, December 1976).

[18] It is rather startling to come across papers on the subject

of unemployment (including those presented at conferences
devoted to our present difficulties) which start off by saying
'I assume the economy is at full employment, or tends strongly
and inevitably to get to that state.'

[19] Since the lectures on which this book is based were given,
a Conservative Chancellor of the Exchequer who is a devout
believer in monetarism has taken over. He has not, however,
hesitated to lecture the trade unions on the need for wage
restraint, or refrained from announcing how tough he will be
in public sector wage bargaining. If the labour market is just
another market (indeed, to be correctly approximated as a
perfect free market), this is a quite futile effort. In what
appears to be an excellent and succinct account of part of the
monetarist approach A. A. Housman states, 'Because of the
non-unique role of the labour market, monetarist analyses pass
over it when considering the disequilibrium dynamics of
inflation.' ('Cripps on wages and the quantity theory – a
monetarist reply', *Cambridge Journal of Economics*, June
1979.)